WHAT I BELIEVE 1

Listening and Speaking about What Really Matters

ELIZABETH BÖTTCHER

PEARSON
Longman

What I Believe 1

Pearson Education, 10 Bank Street, White Plains, NY 10606

Staff credits: The people who made up the *What I Believe 1* team, representing editorial, production, design, and manufacturing, are Eleanor Barnes, John Beaumont, Elizabeth Carlson, Nan Clarke, Stacey Hunter, Amy McCormick, Michael Mone, Rob Ruvo, Keyana Shaw, Debbie Sistino, Paula Van Ells, and Patricia Wosczyk.
Cover design: Patricia Wosczyk
Text design: Wanda España
Cover art: Quint Buchholz
Text composition: Laserwords

Audio and Text Credits: "The Artistry of Hidden Talents," "Seeing in Beautiful, Precise Pictures," "The Importance of Parenting," "The Connection Between Strangers," "A Grown-Up Barbie," "The Hardest Work You Will Ever Do," "Unleashing the Power of Creativity," "The People Who Love You," "Tomorrow Will Be a Better Day," "What Have I Learned?," "We Are Each Other's Business," "A Shared Moment of Trust," *All Copyright © 2008 by Pearson Education. Copyright © 2006 by This I Believe, Inc. Reprinted by permission of Henry Holt and Company, LLC.*

Photo Credits: **Pages iv, 1** Nubar Alexanian; **p. 2** Lebrecht Music and Arts Photo Library/Alamy; **p. 5** Hulton Archive/Getty Images; **p. 10** Quint Buchholz; **pp. iv, 11** Nubar Alexanian; **p. 12** Steve Bloom Images/Alamy; **p. 16** Rosalie Winard Photography; **p. 22** Quint Buchholz; **pp. iv, 23** Nubar Alexanian; **p. 24** Judith Haeusler/Stone/Getty Images; **p. 33** Quint Buchholz, **pp. iv, 34** Jim Conway; **p. 35** Photodisc/Fotosearch; **p. 38** © 2007 The Associated Press; **p. 44** Quint Buchholz; **pp. iv, 45** Nubar Alexanian; **p. 46** Lawrence Lucier/Stringer/Getty Images; **p. 48** Krista Kennell/Zuma/Corbis; **p. 53** Quint Buchholz; **pp. iv, 54** Nubar Alexanian; **p. 55** Design Pics/Fotosearch; **p. 58** Map Resources/Fotosearch; **p. 63** Quint Buchholz; **pp. vi, 64** © 2007 The Associated Press; **p. 65** Bettmann/Corbis; **p. 67** IBM Corporation; **p. 73** Quint Buchholz; **pp. vi, 74** Nubar Alexanian; **p. 75** Ron Chapple/Corbis; **p. 77** © 2007 The Associated Press; **p. 83** Quint Buchholz; **pp. vi, 84** Nubar Alexanian; **p. 85** Corbis; **p. 94** Quint Buchholz; **pp. vi, 95** Nubar Alexanian; **p. 96** (all) John and Eleanor Barnes; **p. 99** Courtesy Elizabeth Deutsch Earle; **p. 104** Quint Buchholz; **pp. vi, 105** Nubar Alexanian; **p. 106** Steve Raymer/Corbis; **p. 108** Printed by permission of the Norman Rockwell Family Agency © 1943 Norman Rockwell Family Entities; **p. 115** Quint Buchholz; **pp. vi, 116** Nubar Alexanian; **p. 117** Shutterstock; **p. 120** Bettmann/Corbis.

Library of Congress Cataloging-in-Publication Data

Böttcher, Elizabeth.
   What I believe 1 : listening and speaking about what really matters / Elizabeth Böttcher.
      p. cm.
   ISBN-13: 978-0-13-233327-6 (student book : alk. paper)
   ISBN-13: 978-0-13-233328-3 (audio cd)
   ISBN-13: 978-0-13-233329-0 (teacher's manual and answer key : alk. paper) 1. English language—Study and Teaching—Foreign speakers. 2. Communicative competence. I. Title: What I believe one. II. Title.
   PE1128.A2B62 2008
   428.3'4—dc22

                                                    2007048559
Printed in the United States of America
3 4 5 6 7—CRK—13 12 11 10 09 08

SCOPE AND SEQUENCE

ACKNOWLEDGMENTS

I would like to thank John Beaumont for laying out the blueprint for this book. His insight, ongoing guidance, and attention to detail were a constant source of clarity. I would also like to express my deep gratitude to Eleanor Kirby Barnes, who is not only a brilliant editor, but also an outstanding teacher. I would also like to thank Stacey Hunter for her patience, dedication, and guidance. I am also grateful to Neil Applebaum and Barbara Sarapata, my colleagues at the American Language Program, for piloting units from *What I Believe 1* and providing such beneficial feedback. Mary Ward, the author of *What I Believe 2*, has been a tremendous source of support, as well. The love and patience of my husband, Lucas and our son, Justin made it possible for me to navigate my way as a first-time author. They are a constant reminder of what I believe.

—*Elizabeth Böttcher*

Pearson Longman gratefully recognizes the cooperation of **Dan Gediman**, producer of *This I Believe*; **Mary Jo Gediman**, *This I Believe* Outreach Director; **Jay Allison**, host and curator of *This I Believe*, and **Denise Cronin** of Henry Holt.

The Publisher also extends special thanks to the following individuals whose comments were instrumental in shaping this series:

Meghan Ackley, University of Texas, Austin, TX; **Jean Correll**, Wheaton High School, Wheaton, MD; **Holly Fernalld**, Niwot High School, Niwot, CO; **Jennifer Gaudet**, Santa Ana School of Continuing Education, Santa Ana, CA; **Lisa Hockstein**, Westchester Community College, Valhalla, NY; **Kate Johnson**, Union County College, Elizabeth, NJ; **Tamara Jones**, Howard Community College, Columbia, MD; **Ronny Kempenich**, Wheaton High School, Wheaton TX; **Sydney Lally**, Quincy High School, Quincy MA; **Kristin Ruopp Mena**, Montgomery Blair High School, Silver Springs, MD; **Kim Newcomer**, University of Washington, Seattle, WA; **Delis Pitt**, Columbia University and New School University, New York, NY; **Theresa Sammarco**, Wootton High School, Rockville, MD; **Kelly Roberts Weibel**, Edmonds Community College, Lynwood, WA; **David Wiese**, New York University, and New School University, New York, NY.

Also, many thanks to research assistant: **John Kay Lee**

PRONUNCIATION	FUNCTION	SPEAKING TASK
Question intonation	Asking for information	Interview a partner about a hidden talent
Reductions: /gonna/, /hafta/, and /hasta/	Describing future plans	Speak about a plan to solve a problem
Regular past tense endings	Describing past events	Tell a story about a time when someone helped you to learn something important
Content word stress in sentences	Making suggestions	Act out a role play about how to reach out to a stranger
Reduction of function words	Discussing habitual actions in the past	Have an informal group discussion about past experiences
Reduction of has and have with present perfect	Describing changes	Give a short speech about how an experience has changed you for the better

	UNIT	TOPIC	LANGUAGE
	UNIT 7 Unleashing the Power of Creativity —Bill Gates	Using creativity and intelligence to make the world a better place	Gerunds
	UNIT 8 The People Who Love You —Cecile Gilmer	Appreciating the true meaning of *family*	Arguing a point: Language for giving opinions, examples, and counter opinions
	UNIT 9 Tomorrow Will Be a Better Day —Josh Rittenberg	Comparing life yesterday and today	Comparatives
	UNIT 10 What Have I Learned? —Elizabeth Deutsch Earle	Making the most of each day	Giving advice: *should, ought to,* and *had better*
	UNIT 11 We Are Each Other's Business —Eboo Patel	Taking responsibility for our actions	Apologizing; Giving explanations and excuses with *had to* and *couldn't*
	UNIT 12 A Shared Moment of Trust —Warren Christopher	Trusting	Present real and unreal conditionals

PRONUNCIATION	FUNCTION	SPEAKING TASK
Linking a final consonant to the next word	Explaining purpose	Explain the purpose of a charitable organization
Thought groups	Arguing a point	Debate the pros and cons of adoption
Stress in compound nouns	Making predictions and comparisons about the future	Make predictions and discuss how life will be different 25 years from now
Corrective stress	Asking for, giving, and receiving advice	Act out a role play for a radio call-in show
Contrastive stress	Making apologies and excuses	Act out a role play in which two people express disappointment, make apologies, and give excuses
Reduction and stress of *can* and *can't*	Sorting alternatives	Participate in a group discussion about what you would do if someone or something you rely on were suddenly not there

UNIT TOUR

Glossary defines important lower-frequency words and expressions to support listening comprehension.

Connect to the Topic prepares students to listen by offering an early opportunity to engage in the topic and anticipate what they will hear in the essay.

UNIT 11

WE ARE EACH OTHER'S BUSINESS
–Eboo Patel

GETTING READY

CD 2 Track 33   Listen and read about the essayist.

Meet Eboo Patel
Eboo Patel is an American Muslim. He is the founder and director of the Interfaith Youth Core. This organization tries to create understanding and respect among people from different backgrounds. Patel believes in pluralism. He believes that people of different ethnic, religious, and cultural groups can live together in peace. He has a copy of Norman Rockwell's picture *Freedom of Worship* hanging on his office wall to remind him of his goals.

105

Connect to the Topic

Discuss this situation with a partner.

Eboo Patel believes that people from different ethnic and religious groups can live together in peace. Imagine this situation: You and a friend are all alone in a school hallway. Suddenly a group of tough school bullies[1] appear. They start insulting and hitting your friend because of his or her religion. What do you do or say?

GLOSSARY

You will hear these words and expressions in the essay. Read their definitions before you listen.

piety /ˈpaɪət̬i/ *n.* showing respect for God and religion

vivid depiction /vɪvɪd dɪptʃʌn/ *adj.+ n.* description that is so clear that it seems real

devout /dɪˈvaʊt/ *adj.* having very strong beliefs, especially religious ones

hovered /ˈhʌvəd/ *v.* stayed close

anti-Semitic (slurs) /æntisɛmət̬ɪk(slɜrs)/ *adj. + n.* (insults) against Jewish people

averted (my) eyes /əˈvɜrtd maɪ aɪz/ *exp.* looked away

Devout Muslims at prayer

[1] powerful people who threaten weaker people

106   UNIT 11

Getting Ready introduces students to the essayist and provides necessary background as a starting point for the exploration of the speaker's core belief.

Listening strategically supports student comprehension by providing purposeful opportunities to listen and explore the content.

Listen for Main Ideas enables students to identify key points in the essays.

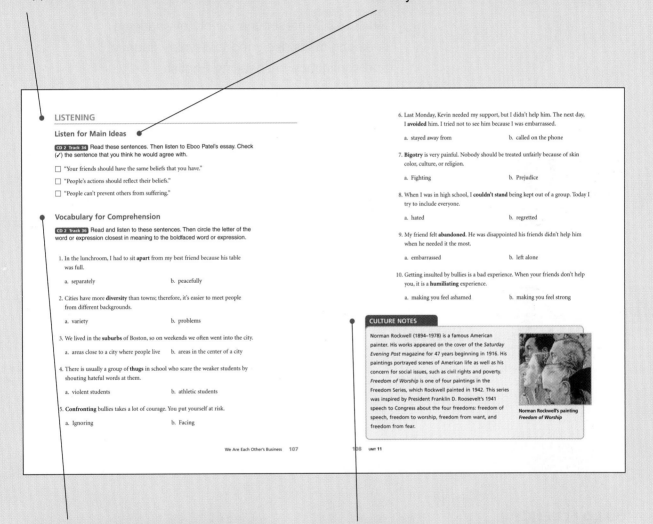

LISTENING

Listen for Main Ideas

CD 2 Track 34 Read these sentences. Then listen to Eboo Patel's essay. Check (✓) the sentence that you think he would agree with.

☐ "Your friends should have the same beliefs that you have."

☐ "People's actions should reflect their beliefs."

☐ "People can't prevent others from suffering."

Vocabulary for Comprehension

CD 2 Track 36 Read and listen to these sentences. Then circle the letter of the word or expression closest in meaning to the boldfaced word or expression.

1. In the lunchroom, I had to sit **apart** from my best friend because his table was full.

   a. separately   b. peacefully

2. Cities have more **diversity** than towns; therefore, it's easier to meet people from different backgrounds.

   a. variety   b. problems

3. We lived in the **suburbs** of Boston, so on weekends we often went into the city.

   a. areas close to a city where people live   b. areas in the center of a city

4. There is usually a group of **thugs** in school who scare the weaker students by shouting hateful words at them.

   a. violent students   b. athletic students

5. **Confronting** bullies takes a lot of courage. You put yourself at risk.

   a. Ignoring   b. Facing

6. Last Monday, Kevin needed my support, but I didn't help him. The next day, I **avoided** him. I tried not to see him because I was embarrassed.

   a. stayed away from   b. called on the phone

7. **Bigotry** is very painful. Nobody should be treated unfairly because of skin color, culture, or religion.

   a. Fighting   b. Prejudice

8. When I was in high school, I **couldn't stand** being kept out of a group. Today I try to include everyone.

   a. hated   b. regretted

9. My friend felt **abandoned**. He was disappointed his friends didn't help him when he needed it the most.

   a. embarrassed   b. left alone

10. Getting insulted by bullies is a bad experience. When your friends don't help you, it is a **humiliating** experience.

    a. making you feel ashamed   b. making you feel strong

CULTURE NOTES

Norman Rockwell (1894–1978) is a famous American painter. His works appeared on the cover of the *Saturday Evening Post* magazine for 47 years beginning in 1916. His paintings portrayed scenes of American life as well as his concern for social issues, such as civil rights and poverty. *Freedom of Worship* is one of four paintings in the Freedom Series, which Rockwell painted in 1942. This series was inspired by President Franklin D. Roosevelt's 1941 speech to Congress about the four freedoms: freedom of speech, freedom to worship, freedom from want, and freedom from fear.

Norman Rockwell's painting
Freedom of Worship

We Are Each Other's Business 107   108 UNIT 11

Vocabulary for Comprehension presents and practices useful, higher-frequency words and expressions to support listening comprehension and classroom interaction on the topic.

Culture Notes and **Background Notes** give insight into historical and cultural references in the essay.

Listen for Details challenges students to listen more closely, go deeper into the topic, and think critically.

Reacting to the Essay invites students to think critically and apply the ideas in the essay to their own experience and beliefs.

Speaking presents a variety of engaging speaking tasks designed to develop fluency and confidence in speaking English.

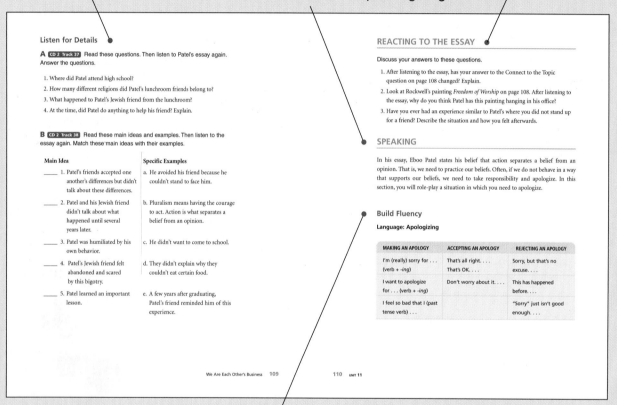

Listen for Details

A CD 2 Track 37 Read these questions. Then listen to Patel's essay again. Answer the questions.

1. Where did Patel attend high school?
2. How many different religions did Patel's lunchroom friends belong to?
3. What happened to Patel's Jewish friend from the lunchroom?
4. At the time, did Patel do anything to help his friend? Explain.

B CD 2 Track 38 Read these main ideas and examples. Then listen to the essay again. Match these main ideas with their examples.

Main Idea	Specific Examples
_____ 1. Patel's friends accepted one another's differences but didn't talk about these differences.	a. He avoided his friend because he couldn't stand to face him.
_____ 2. Patel and his Jewish friend didn't talk about what happened until several years later.	b. Pluralism means having the courage to act. Action is what separates a belief from an opinion.
_____ 3. Patel was humiliated by his own behavior.	c. He didn't want to come to school.
_____ 4. Patel's Jewish friend felt abandoned and scared by this bigotry.	d. They didn't explain why they couldn't eat certain food.
_____ 5. Patel learned an important lesson.	e. A few years after graduating, Patel's friend reminded him of this experience.

REACTING TO THE ESSAY

Discuss your answers to these questions.

1. After listening to the essay, has your answer to the Connect to the Topic question on page 108 changed? Explain.
2. Look at Rockwell's painting *Freedom of Worship* on page 108. After listening to the essay, why do you think Patel has this painting hanging in his office?
3. Have you ever had an experience similar to Patel's where you did not stand up for a friend? Describe the situation and how you felt afterwards.

SPEAKING

In his essay, Eboo Patel states his belief that action separates a belief from an opinion. That is, we need to practice our beliefs. Often, if we do not behave in a way that supports our beliefs, we need to take responsibility and apologize. In this section, you will role-play a situation in which you need to apologize.

Build Fluency

Language: Apologizing

MAKING AN APOLOGY	ACCEPTING AN APOLOGY	REJECTING AN APOLOGY
I'm (really) sorry for . . . (verb + -ing)	That's all right. . . . That's OK. . . .	Sorry, but that's no excuse. . . .
I want to apologize for . . . (verb + -ing)	Don't worry about it. . . .	This has happened before. . . .
I feel so bad that I (past tense verb) . . .		"Sorry" just isn't good enough. . . .

We Are Each Other's Business   109   110   UNIT 11

BUILD FLUENCY

Language teaches and practices important language functions or structures needed for success in the final speaking task.

BUILD FLUENCY

Pronunciation provides instruction and practice in pronunciation, stress, and intonation in preparation for the final speaking task.

Get Ready to Speak guides students through steps to complete the final speaking task.

A: Well, I (5) _____ tell the restaurant manager you weren't here, so they gave our table someone else.

B: Let me tell him we're here now.

Conversation Two

A: You were supposed to call me before 10:00 A.M. and now it's almost 2:00 P.M. What's your excuse this time?

B: Well, I (1) _____ finish some work and lost track of the time.[2]

A: It's always about your work.

B: I really (2) _____ this time. The deadline[3] is tomorrow.

A: (3) _____. You (4) _____ be more organized and not leave everything until the last minute.

B: Uh, I know. (5) _____ not calling you sooner. Do you want to go see a movie tonight?

A: No, (6) _____. I've already made other plans.

Pronunciation: Contrastive Stress

> **CD 2 Track 39** Stress can be moved to show contrast between two words. Stress falls on both words that are being compared. Listen to the example.
>
> EXAMPLE: You were supposed to call me at 10 in the **morning**, not 10 in the **evening**.

PRACTICE Listen and practice saying these sentences with your partner.

1. I wanted to go to the **movies**, but he wanted to go to the **baseball game**.
2. You were supposed to meet me **inside** instead of **outside**.
3. She wanted the red **roses**, not the red **tulips**.

[2] didn't pay attention to the time
[3] day by which something must be completed

4. I didn't order **tea**. I ordered **coffee**.
5. They wanted us to **go**, not **wait**.

Get Ready to Speak

> **TASK**
>
> **Making Apologies and Excuses**
> Prepare a role play with a partner in which you make apologies and excuses. Then present your role play to two other pairs.

1. Work in pairs. Choose a situation. Then brainstorm the details of what caused one person to disappoint the other and why an apology is needed.

Situation 1

Two friends meet three years after they graduate. One of them talks about the time he was discriminated against[4] because of his religion or nationality /ethnic origin. He tells his friend how frightened and lonely he felt because nobody helped him or tried to comfort him.

Situation 2

Two colleagues are working together on a project. One is supposed to finish some work so that the other can complete his or her work. The first person doesn't do what he or she is supposed to, so the second person misses the deadline.

Situation 3

One person is always late. This person has tickets to go to the theater with a friend. She arrives 20 minutes late, and they are not allowed into the performance until the break.

2. Use the information above and the plan on page 114 to create a role play in which two people express disappointment, make apologies and excuses, and accept or reject apologies.

[4] treated unfairly

Useful Expressions boxes offer common expressions in English to increase students' fluency and idiomatic correctness.

Writing gives students an opportunity to recast their ideas in written form, allowing them to go deeper, give personal insights, and receive valuable feedback from their teacher.

Remember to:

• use the expressions from page 110.
• use contrastive stress.

Role Play Plan

A: Express disappointment. Talk about what person B *was supposed to do.*

B: Offer an apology and an excuse. Explain why you *couldn't do* what you were supposed to or what you *had to do.*

A: Accept or reject the apology.

B: If the apology is accepted, thank the person. If the apology is rejected, try to offer more explanation.

A: Close the conversation.

3. Practice your role play in front of another pair. Each pair who listens should make a suggestion about ways the other pair could improve their role play.

> **USEFUL EXPRESSIONS**
>
> **Expressing Disappointment**
>
> You were/weren't supposed to . . .
> Why didn't you . . .
> You should have called.

Speak

Present your role play to two other pairs of students. After you do your role play, listen to the feedback from your audience. See if they believed your excuses and apologies.

WRITING

Read these topics. Choose one to write about.

1. Write about a humiliating or courageous experience that strongly affected you, like Eboo Patel's experience in the lunchroom. Describe the situation in detail and how it affected you.

2. Write about Eboo Patel's belief that action is what separates a belief from an opinion. Do you agree or agree? State your position and explain your reasons.

3. Write an apology letter to the person. Use the information from your role play in the Speaking section on page 113.

> **What do you believe?**
>
> As you listen to the essays in this book, think about your beliefs. Write your own *What I Believe* essay. Follow the steps on pages 127–130.

Speak prompts students when and how to deliver their response to the speaking task.

What do you believe? guides students through the planning, writing and delivery of their own *What I Believe* essay.

THE ARTISTRY IN HIDDEN TALENTS
–Mel Rusnov

GETTING READY

CD 1 Track 2 Listen and read about the essayist.

Meet Mel Rusnov

Mel Rusnov has worked as a civil engineer[1] for over 20 years. However, she also loves playing the piano. In college, she worked in a retirement community.[2] One day she saw a piano in a meeting room and started to play it. Sharing this hidden talent changed her relationship with the residents of the retirement community. As a result, Rusnov believes in developing one's talents.

[1] a person who designs buildings, highways, bus routes, etc.

[2] a place where elderly people live together

Connect to the Topic

Discuss this situation with a partner.

Mel Rusnov believes that sharing talents changes our relationships with others. Imagine that you are at a restaurant with your college roommate. Your roommate suddenly walks over to a piano in the corner of the room and begins to play beautifully. You didn't know that he or she had this hidden talent.

- How do you feel while your roommate is playing the piano? Give three ideas.
- What will you ask your roommate when he or she finishes? Think of two questions.

GLOSSARY

You will hear these words and expressions in the essay. Read their definitions before you listen.

A pianist

ordinary life /ˈɔrdnˌɛri laɪf/ *n.* typical, daily life

pianist /ˈpiænɪst/ *n.* a person who plays the piano

genius /ˈdʒinyəs/ *n.* a person who has a lot of intelligence or a special ability at doing a specific thing

defined by (something) /dɪˈfaɪnd baɪ/ *v.* identified by something you do

keep at (something) /kipˌət/ *v.* continue to do (something)

strip mall /strɪp mɔl/ *n.* a row of small stores with a parking area for cars in front

inhabitants /ɪnˈhæbətənts/ *n.* people who live in a specific place

LISTENING

Listen for Main Ideas

CD 1 Track 3 Read these sentences. Then listen to Mel Rusnov's essay. Circle the letter of the sentence that best describes the main idea.

a. By listening to the piano, people in retirement communities can become happy.

b. Everyone needs good teachers to help them keep at it and improve.

c. When you share your talents with other people, they react differently to you.

Vocabulary for Comprehension

CD 1 Track 5 Read and listen to these sentences. Then match the boldfaced words or expressions with their definitions on page 4.

_c_ 1. I believe in **cultivating** hidden talents. It's important to make time for your talents or hobbies.

____ 2. **Disbelieving**, the residents sat and listened to Rusnov play. They didn't know she was so talented!

____ 3. Rusnov was no longer **invisible to** the residents. After she played, they noticed her and wanted to talk to her.

____ 4. For over twenty years, I was totally **absorbed in** my career. I didn't do anything else.

____ 5. After a long week at the office, I was completely **spent**. I had no energy at all.

____ 6. Steve was my **colleague**. We worked together for nine years.

____ 7. I took music lessons from an **inspiring** teacher. Her lessons were always fun, and I wanted to practice all the time.

____ 8. I'm usually shy in class, but today we were talking about music. I know a lot about it, so I felt **bold**.

____ 9. I can hear my colleagues working in their **cubicles**, but sometimes we don't see one another all day.

____ 10. Playing the piano **transformed** my relationships with my coworkers. Now we talk about work, our personal lives, and our other interests.

a. busy with

b. unnoticed by

c. developing

d. making someone want to do something well

e. being very surprised

f. confident

g. changed

h. small desks or work areas with short walls around them

i. coworker

j. extremely tired

Listen for Details

A CD 1 Track 6 Read these sentences. Then listen to Rusnov's essay again. Did these things happen? Check (✓) the correct box.

	It happened.	It didn't happen.
1. Rusnov earned a college degree in music.	☐	☑
2. When she was younger, Rusnov worked as a waitress at a retirement community.	☐	☐
3. A hardworking civil engineer, Rusnov didn't play the piano for 20 years.	☐	☐
4. At a holiday concert, Rusnov cried when she heard a man with a beautiful voice sing.	☐	☐
5. Inspired by her colleague, Rusnov started taking singing lessons.	☐	☐
6. Rusnov played a Beethoven sonata for strangers in an airport.	☐	☐

B CD 1 Track 7 Read these sentences. Then listen to the essay again. Number the events in the order that they happened.

_____ a. Rusnov started taking piano lessons from an inspiring teacher.

_____ b. After she played, the residents at the retirement community asked her a lot of questions about music and musicians.

_____ c. Rusnov's piano playing transformed the ordinary activity of the travelers at the airport.

_____ d. Rusnov discovered a piano in a room of a retirement community where she worked.

_____ e. Rusnov was surprised to hear her colleague Steve's glorious tenor singing voice.

REACTING TO THE ESSAY

Discuss your answers to these questions.

1. Think about the Connect to the Topic situation on page 2. Have you ever discovered that someone had a special talent or hobby? Did this discovery change your relationship with that person? How?

2. Do you think that Rusnov's life is different now that she develops her talent? Explain.

3. Do you have a "hidden talent?" Do your friends and family members? Explain.

SPEAKING

In her essay, Mel Rusnov states her belief that people are more than just employees or members of a family. She believes that, by cultivating and sharing our talents, our relationships with people change and grow. In this section, you will interview a partner about a hidden talent and present this information to the class.

Build Fluency

Language: *Wh-* Questions

To ask for specific information, use *wh-* questions (information questions). In some *wh-* questions, the question word is the subject. To form these questions, use a question word followed by a verb.

WH- WORD-SUBJECT		
What	are	your favorite hobbies?
Who	was	your teacher?
Who	paid	for your lessons?

In other information questions, the question word is an object or complement. To form these *wh-* questions, begin with the question word followed by a helping verb + subject + main verb.

WH- QUESTION-OBJECT OR COMPLEMENT				
Why	do	you	like	to play the piano?
How long	have	you	played	the piano?
Where	did	you	study	piano?
How	do	you	feel	when you play?
When	do	you	like	to play?

PRACTICE Read the answers to this interview. Then write the questions. Use *what, when, where, how, why,* or *(for) how long* and the correct verb tense.

1. A: _What is your favorite hobby?_____

   B: Baking is my favorite hobby.

2. A: _____

   B: I bake because it's fun, and I really enjoy it.

3. A: _____

   B: I feel happy when I bake for my family and friends.

4. A: _____

   B: I have baked cakes since I was eight years old.

5. A: _____

   B: One of my best memories of baking is when I made my dad a birthday cake.

6. A: _____

   B: He felt so touched that he almost cried.

7. A: _____

   B: I like to bake in my mom's kitchen.

Pronunciation: Question Intonation

CD 1 Track 8 *Wh-* questions usually have falling intonation. Listen to the example.

EXAMPLE:

What is your favorite hobby?

However, when you want someone to repeat information in a *wh-* question, the intonation goes up.

EXAMPLE:

What is your favorite hobby again?

Questions with a *yes* or *no* answer usually have rising intonation.

EXAMPLE:

Do you have any hidden talents or hobbies?

PRACTICE Listen and repeat these questions. You will use them later in the unit.

1. Did you have a special talent or hobby when you were young? What was it?
2. When did you first begin doing it?
3. Did you ever take any lessons? For how long?
4. How did you get interested in this hobby?
5. How does developing your hobby or talent make you feel?
6. Do you have any special memories about this? What are they?
7. Have you kept at your hobby? If not, why did you stop?

Get Ready to Speak

TASK

Asking for Information

Interview a partner about his or her hobby or talent. Then share your partner's information with the class.

1. Work alone. Write five questions to ask your partner about his or her hobbies or talents. Use the questions from the Pronunciation section on page 8 to help you. Plan to ask your partner to describe at least two memories about his or her hobby or talent.

2. Interview your partner. As you interview each other, ask follow-up questions to get more information. To ask follow-up questions, use questions from the Pronunciation section and the Useful Expressions below.

Remember to:

• get your partner to give you as many interesting details as possible.

• take notes.

• use correct question intonation.

USEFUL EXPRESSIONS

Follow-up Questions

Could you explain that a little more?

Could you be a little more specific?

How did you feel when . . . ?

How did other people react when . . . ?

---

3. Prepare and practice your presentation. Use your notes from your interview. Organize the information in an interesting way. Practice giving your presentation as your partner listens and takes notes.

Speak

Present your information on your partner's talent or hobby to the class while your classmates take notes. After each presentation, your classmates will ask follow-up questions.

WRITING

Read these topics. Choose one to write about.

1. Mel Rusnov believes that we need to make time in our busy lives to develop talents and hobbies. What is your reaction to this statement? Explain.

2. Think about the ways Mel Rusnov's hidden talent transformed and connected the people who listened to her playing. Imagine that you are either a resident of the retirement community or a person in the airport lobby. Write a letter to Rusnov describing what you saw and how you felt when she played the piano.

3. Write about one of your own hidden talents or hobbies. You may want to write about the talent you discussed with your partner in the Speaking section.

What do you believe?

As you listen to the essays in this book, think about your beliefs. Write your own *What I Believe* essay. Follow the steps on pages 127–130.

SEEING IN BEAUTIFUL, PRECISE PICTURES
–Temple Grandin

GETTING READY

CD 1 Track 9 Listen and read about the essayist.

Meet Temple Grandin

Temple Grandin is an associate professor of animal science at Colorado State University. She designs facilities[1] for farm animals. Her designs make living and dying as peaceful as possible for the animals. Grandin has autism, a condition that affects her ability to communicate and the way she thinks about the world. Because of her autism, Grandin can only think and learn in very clear, practical[2] ways.

[1] rooms or buildings used for a specific purpose

[2] realistic and useful

Connect to the Topic

Temple Grandin is a practical thinker. What about you? Discuss these questions with a partner.

What would be the most practical way for you to learn about a new machine or piece of technology, such as a computer? Choose one. Explain your choice.

- First read the instruction manual.
- Look at a picture or diagram that shows the parts and how it works.
- "Learn by doing." That is, use the machine and discover things yourself.

GLOSSARY

You will hear these words and expressions in the essay. Read their definitions before you listen.

A mother horse and her foal

Ranching Terms

foal /foʊl/ *n.* a very young horse

ranch /ræntʃ/ *n.* a very large farm where cattle, horses, and sheep are raised

slaughterhouse /ˈslɔtɚˌhaʊs/ *n.* a building where ranch animals are killed

feedlot /ˈfidlɑt/ *n.* a building or area of ground where animals rest and eat to get fatter

cattle /ˈkæt̮l/ *n.* (*non-count*) cows and bulls kept on a farm

corral /kəˈræl/ *n.* an enclosed area for cattle, horses, and sheep

LISTENING

Listen for Main Ideas

CD 1 Track 10 Read these sentences. Then listen to Temple Grandin's essay. Circle the letter of the answer that best completes each sentence.

1. Grandin thinks in _____ and sounds.

   a. words   b. pictures   c. colors

2. Grandin's parents taught her the difference between good behavior and bad behavior by giving her _____.

   a. examples   b. rules   c. ideas

3. Grandin believes in doing _____ things to make the world a better place.

   a. peaceful   b. simple   c. practical

4. Grandin tries to design humane[3] facilities for animals. She believes that when cattle stay calm, they are not _____.

   a. shocked   b. scared   c. hurt

5. Grandin likes thinking in beautiful, precise pictures. She _____ to think like other people.

   a. hopes   b. doesn't want   c. will try

Vocabulary for Comprehension

CD 1 Track 12 Read and listen to these sentences. Then circle the letter of the word or expression closest in meaning to the boldfaced word or expression.

1. It is hard for Temple Grandin to understand **abstract** ideas. She needs to have specific examples.

[3] treated in a kind way

When an idea is **abstract**, it is <u>not</u> based on _____.

   a. thoughts   c. feelings

   b. beliefs   d. real examples

2. She thinks in **images**. For example, if someone says "love," she might see a mother horse and her foal in her mind.

   When you think in **images**, you think in _____.

   a. feelings   c. opinions

   b. pictures   d. language

3. She didn't understand her mother's instructions to "be nice." Those instructions were too **vague** for her to understand without an example.

   When something is **vague**, it is _____.

   a. clear   c. unclean

   b. clean   d. unclear

4. When Grandin's parents gave her specific examples, ideas **made sense** to her. She knew their meaning.

   When something **makes sense**, you can _____ it.

   a. hear   c. write

   b. feel   d. understand

5. Not giving animals a clean place to live, healthy food, and time to rest is **inhumane**.

   When something is **inhumane**, it is _____.

   a. kind and caring   c. useful and effective

   b. cruel and uncaring   d. unrealistic and unsafe

6. Grandin visited 50 different ranches, and she **cataloged** all the things that worked well in each one. This helped her to decide which things she wanted to use in her design.

When you **catalog** groups of things, you _____ them.

a. make a list of

c. make a promise about

b. make a book of

d. make an appointment for

7. She is happy when people tell her that her designs help cattle feel **calm.**

When you feel **calm**, you feel _____.

a. angry

c. worried

b. unhappy

d. relaxed

8. Although Temple Grandin is different, she wouldn't want to **give up** her special way of thinking to be like most people.

When someone **gives up** something, he or she _____ it.

a. stops having or doing

c. agrees to doing or saying

b. tries having or doing

d. starts learning how to do

Listen for Details

A `CD 1 Track 13` Grandin understands ideas through specific examples. Read these main ideas and examples. Then listen to Grandin's essay again. Match these main ideas with their examples.

Main Idea

_____ 1. Grandin thinks in pictures and sounds.

_____ 2. She understands abstract ideas such as "being nice" through specific examples.

_____ 3. She changed the design of slaughterhouses in a practical way.

_____ 4. Grandin is satisfied with her life.

Specific Examples

a. If someone could snap his fingers and change her, she wouldn't change.

b. an image of a mother horse with her foal; the Beatles' song "All You Need Is Love."

c. delivering daffodils (yellow flowers) to a next-door neighbor

d. The animals move through the system more quietly and calmly.

B CD 1 Track 14 Read these questions and statements. Then listen to the essay again. Check (✓) two statements that correctly answer each question.

1. How does Grandin's brain work?

   ☐ a. She hears words in her head.

   ☐ b. She "surfs the Internet" in her brain.

   ☐ c. She surfs the Internet with Google™.

   ☐ d. She sees a clear picture of an example.

2. How did Grandin's parents teach her the difference between good and bad behavior?

   ☐ a. by showing her an example of good behavior

   ☐ b. by sending her to her room to punish her

   ☐ c. by telling her "being nice meant giving daffodils to a neighbor

   ☐ d. by drawing pictures and giving her detailed examples

3. What did Grandin do in the 1970s when she was in her 20s?

   ☐ a. She got married.

   ☐ b. She visited many feedlots and ranches.

   ☐ c. She moved to a ranch for a few years.

   ☐ d. She thought about the meaning of life.

BACKGROUND NOTES

Dr. Temple Grandin is a remarkable woman who has made great achievements. She received her undergraduate degree in psychology and her M.S. and Ph.D. in animal science. She has written five books and appeared on many television and radio programs. There have also been several newspaper and magazine articles written about Dr. Grandin.

Temple Grandin

REACTING TO THE ESSAY

Discuss your answers to these questions.

1. After listening to the essay, has your answer to the question in the Connect to the Topic section on page 12 changed? Explain.

2. Imagine you are speaking to Temple Grandin. What question will you ask her? Why?

3. Grandin believes that by doing practical things we can make the world a better place. Do you think all of us have this ability? Explain.

SPEAKING

In her essay, Temple Grandin states her belief that doing practical things can make the world a better place to live, even for animals. In this section, you will present a plan to solve a problem in your city or school.

Build Fluency

Language: *Have to, Be going to,* and *Will*

Use *have to* + the base form of the verb to discuss things that need to be done to solve a problem.

HAVE TO + BASE FORM OF THE VERB
We **have to buy** more buses.
She **has to change** the bus routes.

Use *be going to* or *will* + the base form of the verb to discuss future plans. When plans have already been decided before the time of speaking, use *be going to*. Use *will* to make an offer or for decisions made at the time of speaking. Use contractions when speaking.

BE GOING TO + BASE FORM OF THE VERB
He**'s going to hire** more bus drivers by the end of the year.
They**'re not going to add** more stops to the bus route.

WILL + BASE FORM OF THE VERB
We**'ll help** you with your homework.
I **won't need** your help after all.

PRACTICE Read the conversation. Then complete the conversation with *have to, be going to,* or *will.* Use Abdul's sentences to help you choose.

Abdul: It's really difficult to get around this city.

Betty: Yeah, we (1) ___*have to*___ improve the bus and subway systems.

Cindy: I agree. We (2) _____ add more buses and subways.

Dan: Right. We also (3) _____ decrease the time between buses and subways.

Abdul: OK, so who wants to be in charge of planning for buses? We need a decision.

Betty: Um, I (4) _____ take care of that.

Abdul: Fantastic! And that leaves the subway. Who wants to be responsible for that?

Cindy: I (5) _____ do that.

Dan: And I (6) _____ help with the subway, too.

Abdul: OK. Let's discuss our plan for the next meeting.

Betty: I (7) _____ get information on the number of buses currently running.

Cindy: And I (8) _____ get that information about the
subways, too.

Pronunciation: Reduction of *Going to* and *Have to*

CD 1 Track 15 When we use *going to* for the future, we usually reduce it to *gonna*. We do not pronounce the word *to*. In the same way, the auxiliaries *have to* and *has to* are reduced to *hafta* and *hasta*. These reduced forms are only used in speech. They are not written. Listen to the examples.

EXAMPLE: I'm *gonna* find out the number of buses running each day.

NOT

I'm *gonna to* find out how many more stops we need.

EXAMPLES: We *hafta* have some new subway lines.

He *hasta* do something about the subways. They're so dirty.

PRACTICE Listen to the sentences. Then practice repeating them with a partner.

1. They have to do something about the food in the cafeteria.

2. The cafeteria is going to offer healthier food next year.

3. The mayor has to solve the city's traffic problems.

4. He's going to discuss the traffic with the city council this week.

5. My sister has to pick up the kids after school every day.

6. Next year they are going to take the bus.

7. I have to work every day this summer.

8. I'm going to take a long vacation at the end of the summer.

Get Ready to Speak

TASK

Describing Future Plans

In groups, prepare a short talk about a practical plan to solve a problem in your city or school.

1. Choose a problem facing your city from the list below or use your own idea. Then brainstorm and list the details of the problem. Read the example worksheet. Write examples.

Problems

- It's difficult to get around in the city.
- It's hard to find a place to live.

- The administrators don't listen to students.
- Food in the school cafeteria is unhealthy.

EXAMPLE:

WORKSHEET

Problem: *It's difficult to get around in the city.*

Details: *The buses and trains don't run very often. The buses are really crowded.*

Practical Solutions: *We are going to suggest adding buses and trains. We also have to have more bicycle lanes so people can . . .*

---

2. Work in groups. Agree on solutions. Use the dialog from the Practice section on page 18 to help you. Complete the worksheet.

```
┌─────────────────────────────────────────────────────────┐
│                      WORKSHEET                           │
│                                                          │
│   Problem:          _____     │
│                                                          │
│                     _____     │
│                                                          │
│                     _____     │
│                                                          │
│   Details:          _____     │
│                                                          │
│                     _____     │
│                                                          │
│                     _____     │
│                                                          │
│   Practical Solutions: _____     │
│                                                          │
│                     _____     │
│                                                          │
│                     _____     │
│                                                          │
│                     _____     │
└─────────────────────────────────────────────────────────┘
```

3. As a group, practice presenting your plan. Divide the responsibility for speaking equally among group members. Each group member could present different pieces of information. Make changes as needed.

Remember to:
- use *be going to* while you are describing your plans.
- use contractions and reduced forms of *going to* and *have to.*

Speak

Present your plan to the class. The class will listen and take notes. Then decide which plan needs to be done first based on the importance or urgency of the problem.

WRITING

Read these topics. Choose one to write about.

1. Write about something practical that you can do to help your family, your class, your community, or the environment. Refer to the list of problems that you wrote about on page 20 to help you.

2. What do you think about Temple Grandin? Write about what you think is interesting about her. Refer to the Reacting to the Essay section on page 17 for ideas.

3. Write a summary of the plan your group presented. Use your notes from the speaking activity to include as many details as possible.

What do you believe?

As you listen to the essays in this book, think about your beliefs. Write your own *What I Believe* essay. Follow the steps on pages 127–130.

THE IMPORTANCE OF PARENTING
–Benjamin Carson

GETTING READY

CD 1 Track 16 Listen and read about the essayist.

Meet Benjamin Carson

Benjamin Carson grew up poor. His mother worked multiple jobs cleaning houses. His dream was to be a doctor. In school, Carson went from being an "A" student to almost failing, and then back to being an "A" student. Today, Carson is a pediatric neurosurgeon. He does brain surgery on children. He believes he is successful because of what he learned from his mother while he was growing up.

Connect to the Topic

Discuss this question with a partner.

Carson believes in the importance of good parenting. Which two personal qualities are most important for a good parent to have? Add your own ideas. Then explain your choices.

caring	hardworking	optimistic	strict[1]	_____
funny	honest	practical	thrifty[2]	_____

A domestic

---

[1] making sure that rules are obeyed
[2] spending money carefully

LISTENING

Listen for Main Ideas

CD 1 Track 17 Read these sentences. Then listen to Carson's essay. Circle the letter of the answer that best completes each sentence.

1. When Carson was a kid, he had to _____ a week.

   a. read two books   b. watch two TV shows   c. write in his diary two days

2. Carson also had to _____.

   a. babysit his brother   b. clean houses   c. write book reports

3. Carson later found out his mother couldn't _____.

   a. drive   b. sew   c. read

4. When Carson first entered high school, he _____ good grades.

   a. wanted to get   b. didn't get   c. didn't care about getting

5. A few years ago, he discovered he had _____.

   a. no money   b. a serious disease   c. no patients

6. Carson's _____ had faith that he would get better.

   a. mother   b. wife   c. father

Vocabulary for Comprehension

CD 1 Track 19 Read and listen to the passage. Then match the boldfaced words and expressions with their definitions on page 26.

As a kid, Carson could not watch more than three (1) **pre-selected** TV shows a week. He had to read two books and (2) **submit** two written reports to his mother. He thought his mother read his reports, but later he found out she was (3) **illiterate** and didn't understand any of them.

In high school, Carson wanted to wear fancy Italian shirts like the other students. His mother gave him all the money she made that week. She told him to buy new shirts—but only after he paid all the bills. When he (4) **got through** paying the bills, there was no money (5) **left over** to buy shirts. Then Carson realized that he couldn't have (6) **immediate** gratification. He had to be patient and work hard for the things he wanted.

Carson worked hard and (7) **eventually** he became a doctor when he grew up. He was a brain surgeon, so he was (8) **faced with** many difficult surgical procedures.

Later, he had a serious illness. Although he was very scared, his mother had faith that he would be (9) **cured**. She believed he would live a long, healthy life. Her strong belief helped Carson deal with his difficult job and his illness.

_____ healed; made healthy   _____ pleasure or reward received

_____ after a long time   _____ very quickly

_____ had to deal with   _____ not used, extra, remaining

_____ finished, completed   _1_ chosen in advance

_____ unable to read or write   _____ give something to someone
                                          (in a formal way)

BACKGROUND NOTES

Some twins are born physically connected, and surgery can separate them. This is very dangerous surgery and takes a great deal of skill. Benjamin Carson is well known for this type of pediatric neurosurgery. Carson began performing this surgery in 1987, when he and a large medical team successfully separated twin boys who were connected at the head.

Formerly conjoined twins

Listen for Details

A CD 1 Track 20 Read these sentences. Then listen to Carson's essay again. Write *T* (true) or *F* (false).

_____ 1. Carson learned that successful people read a lot.

_____ 2. He found out that it's important to wear nice clothes and look good.

_____ 3. Carson realized that working hard is necessary for success.

_____ 4. He discovered that dreams can come true.

_____ 5. Carson learned that faith gives people hope.

B CD 1 Track 21 In his essay, Carson tells us about his mother. Read these sentences. Then listen to the essay again. Check (✓) the topics he mentions.

Mrs. Carson:

☐ 1. spent a lot of time at the Detroit Public Library.

☐ 2. complained about working multiple jobs.

☐ 3. put a roof over her children's heads.

☐ 4. gave them food and clothes even though she didn't earn a lot of money.

☐ 5. believed in immediate gratification.

☐ 6. had strong faith.

☐ 7. was an inspiration.

REACTING TO THE ESSAY

Discuss your answers to these questions.

1. After listening to the essay, has your answer to the Connect to the Topic question on page 24 changed? Explain.

2. Carson believes that there is no job more important than parenting. What is your opinion about this? Do you agree? Is there a more important job? Explain.

3. Do you think Mrs. Carson's life is different today than it was when Benjamin was young? Explain.

SPEAKING

In his essay, Benjamin Carson states he learned important things from his mother that helped him become successful. He believes that there is no job more important than parenting. In this section, you will tell a story about how you learned something important from a parent, family member, or another person.

Build Fluency

Language: Simple Past and Past Progressive

SIMPLE PAST	
To discuss actions, states, and situations that are now completed, use the simple past.	
Regular verbs Add *-d* or *-ed* to the base form of the verb.	EXAMPLE: Carson **watched** two pre-selected TV shows a week.
Irregular verbs Use the irregular past form, such as *was*, *were*, *had*, *went*, *did*, and *said*.	EXAMPLE: Every week, he **read** two books and **wrote** two book reports.
Negative Sentences Use *didn't* + the base form of the verb.	EXAMPLE: Carson **didn't** spend a lot of money on clothes.

PAST PROGRESSIVE	
Use the subject + *was/were* + the base form of the verb + *-ing*. Use the past progressive to show: • an action in the past that was in progress at a specific time. • two actions that were happening at the same time in the past.	EXAMPLES: Mrs. Carson **was working** at 7:30 in the morning. Carson **was reading** while his mom **was cleaning** houses.

SIMPLE PAST AND PAST PROGRESSIVE

Use the simple past with the past progressive to show that one action *interrupted* another action in the past.

When is followed by the simple past.	EXAMPLE: Ben **was writing** a book report *when* Mrs. Carson **told** him to come to dinner.
While is followed by the past progressive.	EXAMPLE: *While* Carson **was paying** the bills, he **realized** his mother was a genius with money.
If two past actions continue at the same time, use past continuous in both parts of the sentence.	EXAMPLE: While my mother **was washing** the dishes, I **was doing** my homework.

PRACTICE Complete these sentences. Use the simple past or past progressive form of the verbs in parentheses.

I'll never forget the time my mom caught me lying. It was a Friday afternoon, and my mom always worked on Fridays, so I (1) _____*decided*_____ (decide) this was a good day to skip school.[3] While my mother (2) _____ (take) a shower, I (3) _____ (call) my best friend, Sue, to make plans. I (4) _____(tell) my mother I was too sick to go to school. Then Sue and I (5) _____ (take) the public bus to the mall. While we (6)_____ (shop), my mother suddenly (7) _____ (appear). What a shock!! When my mother (8) _____ (see) us, she (9) _____ (get) very angry. Mom (10) _____ (bring) Sue and me back to school to talk to the principal. While I (11)

[3] not attend school

_____ (tell) the principal the story, Sue (12) _____ (look) at the floor because she was so embarrassed. That was bad, but the worst part is that my mother will not trust me for a long time because I lied to her.

Pronunciation: Regular Past Tense Endings

CD 1 Track 22 The regular past tense -ed ending can be pronounced three ways: /ɪd/, /t/ and /d/. The pronunciation depends on the last sound in the verb. Listen to the examples.

- If the verb ends with a *t* or *d* sound, -ed is pronounced /ɪd/ and is a separate syllable.

  EXAMPLES: *attended*   *started*

- If the verb ends with a voiceless sound, (such as /p/, /t/, /k/, /f/, /s/, /θ/, /ʃ/, or /tʃ/), -ed is pronounced /t/ and is connected to the last syllable.

  EXAMPLES: *stopped*   *dashed*

- If the verb ends with a voiced sound, (such as /b/, /g/, /dʒ/, /l/, /m/, /n/, /r/, /v/, /ð/, /ŋ/, or a vowel), -ed is pronounced /d/ and is connected to the last syllable.

  EXAMPLES: *changed*   *lived*

A PRACTICE **CD 1 Track 23** Listen and write the words into the correct column in the chart on page 31. Then practice saying the words.

announced	handed	submitted
decided	observed	wanted
dreamed	realized	watched
faced	received	wished

/ɪd/	/t/	/d/
	announced	

B PRACTICE CD 1 Track 24 Listen and practice saying these sentences with a partner. Pay attention to the pronunciation of the *-ed* endings.

1. Ben Carson dreamed of becoming a doctor.
2. Mrs. Carson observed that successful people spend more time reading than watching television.
3. Mrs. Carson announced that her children could only watch two to three preselected television programs during the week.
4. When Carson was in high school, he wanted to wear fancy clothes.

Get Ready to Speak

TASK

Describing Past Events

In groups, tell a story about a time when a family member or another person helped you learn something important. Present your stories in groups.

1. Work alone. Think about lessons you have learned in life and who taught them to you. Important lessons one learns about life might include: always tell the truth, don't wait to do something that you can do right now, save your money because you might need it later, etc. Then choose one of the lessons. Think about whom you learned this lesson from.

Prepare to tell your story by taking notes. Think about these questions:

- Where were you?
- When did this happen?
- Whom were you with?
- What did this person teach you?
- Why was this important for you to learn?
- How has this lesson been helpful to you since that time?

2. Work in pairs. Use your notes to tell a partner a story about a time you learned something important. Practice a few times to get comfortable and to improve the fluency of the presentation. Your partner will ask a question to get more details.

Remember to:

- use the simple past and the past progressive.
- pronounce regular past tense endings /ɪd/, /t/, and /d/.

USEFUL EXPRESSIONS

Starting a story

I'll never forget when . . .

I remember when . . .

Did I tell you about the time . . . ?

Speak

Get together with another pair. Tell your story. The others in the group will take notes on each story. Then ask questions to get more information. Add this information to your notes.

WRITING

Read these topics. Choose one to write about.

1. Ben Carson believes there is no job more important than parenting. What are some lessons he learned from his mother? Refer to your answers from the Listen for Details section on page 27. Explain what he learned, and give an example from Carson's essay.

2. Write about a time someone helped you to learn an important lesson. Use your notes from your presentation in the Speaking section on page 31 to help you organize your details.

3. Ben Carson's mother had an important influence on his life. She was his role model.[4] Write about someone who has been a role model for you. Who is this person? What qualities made him or her a good role model? Explain.

What do you believe?

As you listen to the essays in this book, think about your beliefs. Write your own *What I Believe* essay. Follow the steps on pages 127–130.

[4] someone you admire and try to behave like

UNIT 4

THE CONNECTION BETWEEN STRANGERS
–Miles Goodwin

GETTING READY

CD 1 Track 25 Listen and read about the essayist.

Meet Miles Goodwin

In 1970, Miles Goodwin was a young soldier returning to the United States from the unpopular war in Vietnam. Sitting by himself on the airplane, he felt lonely. Suddenly, a young girl appeared, smiled, and gave him a magazine. He was very grateful[1] for her small act of kindness. Many years later, Goodwin still believes her gesture of kindness greatly influenced his life.

[1] thankful

34

Connect to the Topic

Discuss this situation with a partner.

Goodwin believes kindness connects strangers. Think of a time when a stranger did something nice for you. Complete the chart. Then compare your notes with a partner's.

Where were you?	
What did the person do?	
How did you feel?	

LISTENING

Listen for Main Ideas

CD 1 Track 26 Read the sentence and the adjectives below. Then listen to Miles Goodwin's essay. Circle the letter of each adjective that correctly completes the sentence. There may be more than one answer. Explain your choices.

According to the essay, Goodwin felt _____ by the young girl's gesture.

   a. surprised   b. angered   c. inspired   d. pleased

Vocabulary for Comprehension

CD 1 Track 28 Read and listen to these sentences. Then circle the letter of the word or expression closest in meaning to the boldfaced word or expression.

1. When you speak to someone, it's important to **make eye contact**. You can learn a lot from a person's eyes.

   a. look directly at someone   c. be completely honest

   b. appear intelligent   d. have an interesting idea

2. Other soldiers **warned** him about returning home from Vietnam. Some people were very upset about the war.

   a. explained how to do   c. told someone about something
      something difficult   good that was going to happen

   b. explained the reasons for   d. told someone about something
      doing something   bad that might happen

3. Many people didn't like the Vietnam War. They felt **hostile** toward Vietnam veterans. They were upset with the government, too.

   a. sad   c. sorry

   b. angry   d. thankful

4. On the airplane, Goodwin felt lonely. No one was sitting in the seat next to him. This made his feeling of **isolation** worse.

   a. enjoyment

   b. being alone

   c. being wrong

   d. being ill

5. After the girl walked away, Goodwin **wept**. He turned to the window so that nobody could see the tears falling from his eyes.

   a. cried

   b. smiled

   c. frowned

   d. slept

6. Since the time the little girl helped Goodwin, he has **followed her example** and tried, in different ways, to help people he did not know.

   a. been very confident

   b. done the same for others

   c. looked for other examples

   d. told people about what she did

7. Although Goodwin will never know why this girl **reached out to**[2] him, he is thankful that she did.

   a. spoke to

   b. offered help or kindness to

   c. looked at

   d. sat next to

8. Now that she is grown up, Goodwin hopes that she continues **to touch** other people's lives with her kindness.

   a. hold

   b. feel

   c. influence

   d. thank

9. He thinks of that girl's kindness again and again. Her gesture of kindness to a tired, scared, and lonely soldier has **echoed** in his life ever since that day.

   a. been absent

   b. caused pain

   c. weakened him

   d. come back repeatedly

---

[2] *extended a hand to* is also used in the essay. It means the same as *reached out to.*

The Vietnam War lasted from 1954–1975. The United States was involved from 1961–1972. This was the longest and most unpopular military conflict in American history. The United States joined the South Vietnamese against the North Vietnamese. More than a million Vietnamese, many of whom were not soldiers, died. Over 50,000 Americans lost their lives. This war is still a topic of disagreement today.

Americans protesting the Vietnam War

Listen for Details

A CD 1 Track 29 Read these sentences. Then listen to Goodwin's essay again. Circle the letter of the answer that best completes each sentence.

1. At the time, Goodwin was returning home to _____ after a year in Vietnam.

   a. Dallas, Texas   b. Oakland, California   c. San Francisco, California

2. People warned Goodwin that Vietnam veterans were _____ many Americans at the time.

   a. looking for   b. liked by   c. unpopular with

3. He did not expect a hometown _____ on his return.

   a. parade   b. party   c. celebration

4. At first, Goodwin felt _____ as he sat on plane.

   a. humble and grateful   b. lonely and isolated   c. afraid and confused

5. When the girl gave him the magazine, he felt _____.

   a. foolish   b. scared   c. touched

6. He is _____ that the girl remembers giving him the magazine long ago.

   a. confident   b. unsure   c. hopeful

B `CD 1 Track 30` In his essay, Goodwin talks about his feelings. How did he show these feelings? Listen to the essay again. Complete the chart.

Feelings	How He Showed His Feelings
isolated	*He sat by himself.*
touched	
grateful	

REACTING TO THE ESSAY

Discuss your answers to these questions.

1. Reaching out to someone benefits both people involved. When one person extends a hand to another person, how does the person receiving the help feel? How does the person reaching out feel? Give an example.

2. Think about the opposite situation you discussed in the Connect to the Topic section on page 35. Have you ever reached out and made a connection with a stranger? Where were you? What did you do you?

3. It is not always easy to reach out to strangers. Why is it sometimes difficult? Give as many reasons as you can. Give examples.

SPEAKING

In his essay, Miles Goodwin states his belief that even strangers can connect when they reach out to one another. In this section, you will read about a situation and make suggestions about ways to reach out to a stranger.

Build Fluency

Language: *Could, Let's, Why not . . . ?, Why don't we/you . . . ?*

To make suggestions, use *could, let's, why not,* or *why don't we/you* + the base form of the main verb.

SUGGESTIONS IN STATEMENTS AND QUESTIONS	
Statements Use *could* and *let's* in statements. Using *let's* includes the speaker in the suggestion.	EXAMPLES: You **could** give him this magazine to read. **Let's** smile at that soldier sitting over there. He looks pretty sad.
Questions Use *why not* and *why don't we* or *why don't you* in questions.	EXAMPLES: **Why not** take my old books to sick people in the hospital? Since you're baking, **why don't you** make some cupcakes for Miles's party?

PRACTICE Complete the dialogs with a suggestion. Use the word(s) in parentheses.

1. A: My best friend just broke up with her boyfriend, and she's really depressed.

   B: *You could introduce her to your friend, Raul* _____. (could)

2. A: I've eaten a lot of greasy food lately, and I've gained 10 pounds!

   B: _____? (why don't you)

3. A: My parents haven't seen a movie in a long time.

   B: _____. (let's)

4. A: Mary and John have been home for three days.

   B: _____? (why not)

5. A: I don't know what to wear tonight. Nothing looks good on me.

   B: _____. (could)

6. A: We haven't eaten Korean food for a long time.

   B: _____. (why don't we)

Pronunciation: Stressing Content Words

CD 1 Track 31 Stress content words (nouns, main verbs, and words that have important meaning) in a statement or question. Pronounce them with heavier stress and on a higher pitch.[3] Listen to the examples.

EXAMPLES:

Let's **buy Jane** some **flowers**.

We could **give** him a **ride** to the **train**.

Why don't we **offer** to **walk** his **dog** for him?

CD 1 Track 32 PRACTICE Listen to the first lines in the dialogs from the Practice exercise on page 40. Circle the content words. Then practice the dialogs with a partner.

EXAMPLE:

1. My best friend just broke up with her boyfriend, and she's really depressed.

---

[3] tone

Get Ready to Speak

Making Suggestions

In pairs, prepare a role play. Make suggestions about how to reach out to a stranger in one of the situations. Decide on a plan of action. Then present your role play to the class.

1. Work in pairs. Choose one of these situations, or use one of your own. Brainstorm three things you could do to help the person in the situation you chose.

Situation 1

Your neighbor is an elderly man whose wife died recently. You don't know him very well, but you *do* know that he and his wife were married for sixty years. His daughter came to stay with him for a month after his wife died, but now he is alone with his dog. He spends a lot of time inside his house.

Situation 2

Your classmate who arrived in the United States three weeks ago has been absent for a week. This is her first time away from home, and she misses her family and friends. She lives in the dormitory but doesn't have a roommate. She is very hardworking and likes watching movies.

2. Use your suggestions to create a role play. Remember to:

- use *could, why not, let's,* and *why don't we* as you make your suggestions.
- speak with a heavier stress and a higher pitch for content words than for other words.

Role Play Plan

A: Explain the problem to B.

B: Offer three suggestions of ways to reach out.

A: Agree, disagree, or suggest an alternative.

A and B: Continue your discussion until you reach an agreement on a plan of action.

USEFUL EXPRESSIONS	
Agreeing	**Disagreeing Politely and Suggesting an Alternative**
Yeah, that's a good idea.	I'm not sure about that.
Sure. Great idea!	That's a good idea, but . . .
Definitely!	Why don't we . . . instead.

3. Practice your role play in front of another pair. Each pair who listens should make a suggestion about ways the pair speaking could improve their role play. When making suggestions consider these questions:

- Did the pair speak loudly and slowly enough?
- Did they stress the content words?
- Was the situation of the person who needed help clear?
- Were the ways of reaching out clear?

Speak

Present your role play to the class. The class will take notes and then discuss the suggestions made in the role play.

WRITING

Read these topics. Choose one to write about.

1. Imagine that you are the person who <u>received</u> the help in your role play. Write a thank-you letter to the person who extended a hand to you. End the letter by making a suggestion of something you could do to continue the relationship.

2. Write about a time when a stranger did something nice for you. What was the situation? How did you react? What happened as a result? Use your discussion from the Connect to the Topic section on page 35 to help you organize your ideas.

3. Write your thoughts on why it is sometimes hard to reach out to strangers. Include examples. Use your discussion from the Reacting to the Essay section on page 39 to help you support your thesis.

What do you believe?

As you listen to the essays in this book, think about your beliefs. Write your own *What I Believe* essay. Follow the steps on pages 127–130.

A GROWN-UP BARBIE
–Jane Hamill

GETTING READY

CD 1 Track 33 Listen and read about the essayist.

> ### Meet Jane Hamill
> Jane Hamill is a fashion designer who owns a clothing boutique in Chicago, Illinois. She has lived the life she dreamed of since childhood, a life inspired by her favorite toy—Barbie®.[1] She used her imagination to make clothes for her dolls as a young girl. As a young adult, she studied fashion design in New York and Paris. Hamill believes that imagination can make our dreams come true.

[1] a best-selling fashion doll, first sold in 1959

Connect to the Topic

Read the sentence. Then discuss the questions with a partner.

As a child, Jane Hamill's favorite toy was her Barbie doll.

- What toys are popular today?
- Why do you think they are popular?

GLOSSARY

You will hear these words and expressions in the essay. Read their definitions before you listen.

Malibu Barbie®

Barbie® Terms

accessories /ək'sɛsəriz/ *n.* additional clothes or toys to go with Barbie

camper /'kæmpɚ/ *n.* a car or bus that has beds and cooking equipment

outfits /'aʊt ˌfɪtz/ *n.* a set of clothes worn together

Ken® /kɛn/ *n.* a male doll sold as Barbie's boyfriend

beauty contests /'byuṭi kən 'tɛst/ *n.* competitions determining the most beautiful woman

a puff piece /ə pʌf pis/ *idiom* a report about something or someone given too much praise

sleeve /sliv/ *n.* the part of a shirt or jacket that covers your arm

Malibu Barbie /'mæləbu 'bɑrbi/ *n.* a Barbie doll dressed for the beach

LISTENING

Listen for Main Ideas

CD 1 Track 34 Read the sentence and endings. Then listen to Jane Hamill's essay. Circle the letter of the answer that best completes the sentence.

Hamill's role model was Barbie because . . .

a. Barbie was beautiful and popular.

b. Barbie had a boyfriend named Ken.

c. Barbie was independent and smart.

Vocabulary for Comprehension

CD 1 Track 36 Read these words and their definitions. Use them to complete the sentences that follow. Then listen to the sentences and check your answers.

body issues *pl. n.* worries or concerns about how our bodies look

dusty *adj.* covered by light, powdery dirt

fancy *adj.* special, expensive, and fashionable

feminist *n.* someone who believes in equal rights for women

idols *n.* heroes

(something) **is all about** (something) *idiom* is the important or main part of

make a difference *idiom* are important

moron *n.* someone who is very foolish

prosecutor *n.* lawyer

1. Hamill considers herself a _____*feminist*_____. She's pleased to see that more women are becoming doctors, lawyers, and engineers.

2. Sometimes Hamill feels like a _____ because she believes in living like Barbie. Many people think of Barbie as being unintelligent.

3. For kids, playing _____ using their imaginations. They love to pretend to be other people and be in other places.

4. I found some of my old toys in a closet at my mom's house. They were _____ because nobody uses or cleans them.

5. She often went to _____ dinner parties. Everyone wore their best outfits.

6. Superman, Batman, and Spider-Man have been children's _____ for a long time. Children admire their powers and skills.

7. During a trial, a _____ tries to prove to the jury that someone is guilty.

8. If you want a job, wear nice clothes to your interview. Your clothes _____ and can influence the opinions of the people interviewing you.

9. We all have _____ because we are rarely satisfied with our physical appearance.

BACKGROUND NOTES

In her essay, Jane Hamill mentions these important women:

Georgia O'Keeffe (1887–1986): A female painter at a time when most painters were male. O'Keeffe's paintings expressed her personal feelings and ideas.

Gloria Steinem (1934–): A journalist and a leader in the women's rights movement in the United States. She founded *Ms.* magazine, the first national women's magazine run by women.

Madeleine Albright (1937–): The first U.S. female secretary of state, the highest ranking female position in the U.S. government, during William Jefferson Clinton's presidency.

Gloria Steinem

Listen for Details

A CD 1 Track 37 Read these sentences. Then listen to Hamill's essay again. Write *T* (true) or *F* (false).

_____ 1. Barbie's accessories such as her airplane, apartment building, and camper were expensive.

_____ 2. Hamill pretended Barbie and her friends were married to airplane pilots, nurses, and fashion designers.

_____ 3. Her Barbie entered beauty contests, got married, and had children.

_____ 4. Hamill doesn't like clothes even though she's a fashion designer.

_____ 5. Hamill hopes her clothes help her customers feel confident.

_____ 6. When Hamill was a little girl, she thought she looked like Barbie.

B CD 1 Track 38 Read these questions. Then listen to the essay again. Write your answers to the questions.

1. Hamill liked to pretend Barbie traveled. Where did Hamill pretend that Barbie went? What did Barbie do in these places?

2. When Hamill was a little girl, what was Barbie about for her? What adjectives does Hamill use to describe herself as a woman?

3. Why does Hamill think her husband's profession as a prosecutor is a worthwhile[2] career?

4. At the end of her essay, which three adjectives does Hamill use to describe why Barbie was her idol as a child?

REACTING TO THE ESSAY

Discuss your answers to these questions.

1. Small children like to pretend that they are grown-ups when they play. They imagine they are doctors, firefighters, teachers, or astronauts, for example. Jane Hamill used to pretend she was Barbie. Whom did you pretend to be? Why?

2. Hamill states that many people today have "body issues." Why is there so much pressure to be thin today? Where do these ideas come from?

[2] meaningful

3. Were you surprised that Barbie was Hamill's idol as a child? Who were your childhood idols? Describe them.

SPEAKING

In her essay, Jane Hamill states her belief in her imagination. This was the result of playing with a toy, her Barbie® doll, which helped her to imagine many things for herself. In this section, you will have a discussion about a favorite toy you had when you were a child.

Build Fluency

Language: *Used to*

Used to describes actions that happened repeatedly in the past but no longer happen.

***USED TO* + BASE FORM OF THE VERB**	
	EXAMPLES:
Use *used to* + the base form of the verb.	Jane Hamill **used to play** with Barbie.
To form the negative, use *didn't use to*. To form questions, use *did* or a question word + *did . . . use to*	Hamill **didn't use to play** with her Ken doll. *Who* **did you use to play** with?
Follow *used to imagine/pretend* with a *that* clause (*that* + subject + simple past).	Hamill *used to pretend* **that she was** a fashion designer.

PRACTICE Read this conversation. There are nine mistakes in all. Find the mistakes and correct them.

A: Who did you use to pretend that you ~~are~~ *were* when you were a child?

B: I used imagine that I was a teacher.

A: Really? What did you used to do?

B: Well, I used to taught my imaginary class different subjects.

A: Where did you use to do that?

B: I imagined that my bedroom was a classroom, and I collect extra handouts from my teacher.

A: What for?

B: Um, I imagined that my students are sitting in a circle, and I handed out papers to teach a lesson.

A: What else did you use to do with your class?

B: Mm, I also used to take my class on imaginary field trips. I used to pretend that my bicycle was a bus, and we go to different places.

A: How did you feel when you play teacher?

B: I felt great!

A: How come?

B: Well, I really admired my teachers, so I guess I used to wanted to be just like them.

Pronunciation: Reduction of Function Words

CD 1 Track 39 We stress content words when we speak (see the Pronunciation section on page 41). We usually reduce function words (words needed for grammar but not for meaning) by reducing the vowels to /ə/. Listen to the examples.

EXAMPLES:

I learned <u>to</u> sew so I could make outfits <u>for</u> Barbie and <u>her</u> friends.

My Barbie didn't enter beauty contests, get married, <u>or</u> have children. She went <u>to</u> Paris and New York <u>for</u> fancy dinners <u>and</u> meetings.

PRACTICE Listen to the dialog from the Practice exercise on pages 50–51. Circle the reduced function words. Then practice the dialog with a partner.

Get Ready to Speak

TASK

Discussing a Favorite Toy or Game

In groups, discuss a favorite toy you had when you were a child. Talk about what it was, how you played with it, and why you liked it.

1. Work alone. For three minutes, brainstorm your favorite toys, how you played with them, and why you liked them. Then choose one to talk about.

Toy	How you played with it	Why you liked it

2. Work in pairs. Take turns discussing your favorite childhood toys. Ask follow-up questions.

Remember to:

• use *imagine/pretend* + *that* clause and *used to*.

• reduce function words and stress content words in your sentences.

USEFUL EXPRESSIONS

Short Follow-up Questions

How come? (Why?)

What for? (What's the reason for that?)

Like what? (What is an example?)

Speak

Get together with another pair. Then ask questions to get more information about your partner's favorite toy. Take notes. Get as many details as possible. After the discussion, present a summary to the class.

WRITING

Read these topics. Choose one to write about.

1. Write about Jane Hamill's belief that you can do something if you can imagine yourself doing it. In other words, you can make your dream come true. Do you agree or disagree with her? Explain.

2. Write about your discussion from the Speaking section on pages 52–53. Describe what you or a group member used to pretend and how you used to play.

3. Hamill says that helping her customers feel confident makes a difference to her. Write about something you do that you think is worthwhile.

What do you believe?

As you listen to the essays in this book, think about your beliefs. Write your own *What I Believe* essay. Follow the steps on pages 127–130.

UNIT 6

THE HARDEST WORK YOU'LL EVER DO
–Mary Cook

GETTING READY

CD 1 Track 40 Listen and read about the essayist.

> ### Meet Mary Cook
>
> Mary Cook lives in a small town of about 350 people in Alaska. She has several jobs: she works for an air taxi company,[1] she is responsible for the town mail, and she runs the town's only coffeehouse. She has always been competent[2] and independent. However, after a tragic accident, Cook learned to depend more on others. She believes she is now a stronger person.

[1] a company that uses small airplanes as taxis
[2] capable

Connect to the Topic

Discuss your answers with a partner.

Mary Cook believes that she is now a stronger person than she used to be. Are you different than you were five years ago? Look at these words. Underline two words that described you then. Circle two words that describe you now. Add your own adjectives, if necessary. Then compare your ideas with a partner's.

confident   independent   sensitive   _____

curious   lazy   strong   _____

GLOSSARY

You will hear these words and expressions in the essay. Read their definitions before you listen.

A woman shoveling her driveway

snowplow /'snouplau/ *n.* equipment used for pushing snow off the roads

driveway /draɪvweɪ/ *n.* the road for cars that runs between one house and a street

(side)walk /'saɪdwɔk/ *n.* the place on the side of a street where people can walk

shovel /'ʃʌvəl/ *v.* remove snow (for example, from a driveway or a sidewalk)

good Samaritans /gʊd səˈmærətənz/ *n.* people who help others

sentiments /'sɛntəmənts/ *n.* feelings

humility /hyuˈmɪləti/ *n.* not being overly proud of oneself or one's actions; **humble** *(adj.)*

surrender /səˈrɛndɚ/ *n.* accept something you have been fighting against

LISTENING

Listen for Main Ideas

CD 1 Track 41 Read these sentences. Then listen to Mary Cook's essay. Check (✓) the sentence that you think Cook would agree with.

☐ 1. "People always ask me to help them because I'm very independent."

☐ 2. "I'm a better person now because I can accept help from others."

☐ 3. "I'm proud that I will never need help from anyone."

Vocabulary for Comprehension

CD 1 Track 43 Read and listen to the thank-you letter. Then match the boldfaced words or expressions with their definitions on page 57.

Dear Kathy,

I can't believe that four months have passed since Jon's tragic accident. I have been in so much pain. Dealing with my **grief** has been very difficult. The hardest thing has been **being open to** help from friends like you. I've always **taken** so much **pride in** my independence.

I remember the first time I saw some neighbors shoveling snow for me. The snow had really **piled up** outside. I was **startled** to see them because I rarely asked people to **do me favors** like shoveling, cooking, and cleaning. But at that time, I could barely do anything for myself—and I was **mortified** by this fact. So many friends were helping me. I had a lot of trouble accepting the support of you good Samaritans.

Kathy, in your sweet way, you told me to stop crying and accept their help and support. You told me that it wasn't a **chore** to cook or clean for me. Thank you so much for your support. I will always feel **gratitude** for you and all those who supported me during those **dark days**.

Love,

Mary

_b_   1. grief   a. ashamed

_____ 2. be open to   b. sadness because someone has died

_____ 3. been proud of   c. help me out

_____ 4. piled up   d. very surprised; very shocked

_____ 5. startled   e. formed a large amount

_____ 6. do me favors   f. thankfulness

_____ 7. mortified   g. unpleasant job

_____ 8. chore   h. very sad times

_____ 9. gratitude   i. willing to accept

_____ 10. dark days   j. felt very pleased with being or doing

                                   things a certain way

Listen for Details

A **CD 1 Track 44** Read these sentences. Then listen to Cook's essay again. Number the events in the order that you hear them. The first one has been done for you.

_____ a. Cook became more grateful and humble.

_1_ b. Cook's fiancé fell off the roof.

_____ c. She just sat on the couch and watched the snow pile up.

_____ d. She worried about returning her neighbors' kindness.

_____ e. Members of her community began helping her.

_____ f. Friends told her that they felt good helping her.

B **CD 1 Track 45** In her essay, Cook talks about her feelings. How did she describe her behavior? Look at the chart and then listen to the essay again. Match her feelings with her descriptions of how she behaved. Write the letter on the line.

Feelings	How She Behaved
_____ 1. mortified	a. She just sat on the couch.
_____ 2. lazy	b. She accepted help and thanked people.
_____ 3. free	c. She wanted to crawl on the floor.

BACKGROUND NOTES

Alaska is the largest state in the United States. It is the same size as France, England, Italy, and Spain put together. Air taxis are a common means of transportation in Alaska because the state is so big.

Alaska is also the northernmost state in the United States. It is located in the far northwest part of North America. Nearly one-third of Alaska is inside the Arctic Circle. As a result, it gets a lot of snow. Winters, like those Mary Cook talks about, last from four to five months a year.

REACTING TO THE ESSAY

Discuss your answers to these questions.

1. Before the accident, Cook says she rarely asked for help or favors. Do you think asking for help is a sign of weakness? Is it ever seen as a sign of weakness in your culture? Why?

2. Cook says that there is "strength in surrender." That is, people can become stronger by accepting a difficult situation. Do you agree? Give an example.

3. Think again about the question in the Connect to the Topic question on page 55. You described a way that you have changed. Did something happen that made you change? Explain.

SPEAKING

In her essay, Mary Cook states that freedom comes from facing your worst fears. Since she has learned to accept help from others, she believes she has changed for the better. In this section, you will plan and present a short speech about how you have changed as a result of a specific event in your life.

Build Fluency

Language: Present Perfect

THE PRESENT PERFECT	
To form the present perfect, use *have / has (not)* + the past participle.	EXAMPLES: Mary Cook **has learned** (that) she doesn't have to do everything herself.
Use contractions when speaking.	Mary**'s changed** for the better.
To show actions that started in the past and continue into the present, use the present perfect. Use *for* to show a period of time. Use *since* to show a point in time.	EXAMPLES: Cook **has been** responsible for the mail *for* many years. She **has been** responsible for the mail *since* she was young.
To show actions in the past when the specific time is not important, use the present perfect.	EXAMPLE: Cook **has changed** her ideas about independence.
<u>Note</u>: To discuss actions completed at a specific time in the past, use the simple past.	EXAMPLE: It **snowed** for almost a week *last year*.

PRACTICE Circle the words that correctly complete each sentence. Use the context to help you.

Rose (1) (has lived / lived) in three countries: France, Germany, and the United States. First, she (2) (has spent / spent) a year living with a French family. That year, Rose (3) (has met / met) and (4) (has married / married) Lucas in Paris. Rose and Lucas (5) (have been married / were married) for many years now. Since then, she (6) (has traveled / traveled) to other European countries such as Spain, Italy, and Germany. From 1999 to 2007, Rose and Lucas (7) (has lived / lived) in Germany. These days, Rose is back in the United States. Since her time in Europe, she (8) (has become / became) aware of other cultures. She (9) (has taught / taught) German at a local high school for a year.

Pronunciation: Reduction of *Has* and *Have* with Present Perfect

CD 1 Track 46 In the present perfect, the sounds of *has* and *have* are sometimes reduced. *Has* is pronounced like [ɪz] or [z]. Listen to the examples.

EXAMPLES: Rose's lived in Paris. (Rozɪz lived in Paris.)

Jon's worked there for ten years. (Jonz worked there for ten years.)

After a pronoun, *have* is pronounced like [v].

EXAMPLES: We've worked here for ten years. (Wev worked here for ten years.)

You've been away for a long time. Welcome home. (Youv been away for a long time. Welcome home.)

After a noun, *have* is pronounced like [əv] (like the word *of*).

EXAMPLES: The children have studied German. (The childrenəv studied German.)

Gloria and Rob have never taken a vacation. (Gloria and Robəv never taken a vacation.)

A `CD 1 Track 47` PRACTICE Listen to these sentences. Circle the letter of the one you hear.

1. a. She's lived in Paris.   b. She lived in Paris.
2. a. The students left.   b. The students have left.
3. a. Josh changed a lot.   b. Josh has changed a lot.
4. a. We cooked dinner.   b. We've cooked dinner.
5. a. They visited Seoul.   b. They've visited Seoul.

B PRACTICE Say the sentences above with a partner. Decide which sentence your partner says.

Get Ready to Speak

TASK

Describing changes

Prepare a 2–3 minute speech about how you have changed as a result of an event in your life. Present your speech in groups.

1. Work in pairs. Brainstorm life-changing events. Add your ideas to the list.

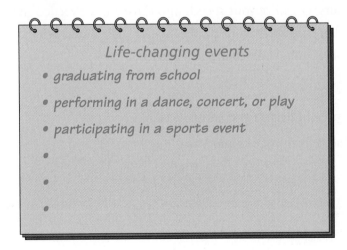

Life-changing events
- graduating from school
- performing in a dance, concert, or play
- participating in a sports event
-
-
-

2. Work alone. Choose an event from the list. Complete the chart.

What happened?	
When did this happen?	
How old were you?	
Where were you?	
Who was there?	
How did you feel?	
Why was this event important?	
How have you changed since this event? (Give 2 examples)	• _I've become accustomed to living away from home._ • _____ • _____

3. Work in pairs. Organize your speech into three parts. Practice giving your speech with a partner. As your partner speaks, take notes. What do you want more details about? Make changes as needed.

Remember to:

• use the present perfect and simple past.
• use reduced forms of *has* and *have*.

USEFUL EXPRESSIONS	
Informal Speech Openers	**Informal Speech Closers**
• Good morning / afternoon / evening! • I'd like to tell you about . . . • I'd like to share a story with you.	• Finally, • To finish up, • Thanks for listening / your attention.

Speak

Work in groups. Take turns presenting your speeches. Group members will ask at least one question and tell each speaker about something they found interesting.

WRITING

Read these topics. Choose one to write about.

1. Mary Cook was surprised to learn that freedom comes from facing one's worst fear and accepting the situation. Describe how Cook faced her fear and changed for the better.

2. Write about the life-changing event you gave your speech about. Describe the event and give important details. Include ideas from your group's questions about your speech.

3. Write about one of your classmate's life-changing experiences. Why did you choose this person's experience, and what did you learn from it?

What do you believe?

As you listen to the essays in this book, think about your beliefs. Write your own *What I Believe* essay. Follow the steps on pages 127–130.

UNIT 7

UNLEASHING THE POWER OF CREATIVITY
–Bill Gates

GETTING READY

CD 2 Track 2 Listen and read about the essayist.

Meet Bill Gates

Bill Gates, the chairman of Microsoft, is a man with a vision[1] of computers changing the world. Gates feels that computers help us "solve problems that even the smartest people couldn't solve on their own." For Gates, computers are just one way that we can use our creativity and intelligence to improve the world. He and his wife are looking for creative solutions to improve people's lives worldwide.

---

[1] dream of or view of the future

Connect to the Topic

Discuss these questions with a partner.

Bill Gates had a vision of computers changing people's lives. How do you use computers in your daily life? Think of three ways. Do computers help you be more creative? How?

Computers in the 1980s were clunky.

LISTENING

Listen for Main Ideas

CD 2 Track 3 Read these sentences. Then listen to Bill Gates' essay. Write *T* (true) or *F* (false).

_____ 1. Bill Gates' life changed the first time he sat down at a computer.

_____ 2. Long ago, Gates and Paul Allen had a vision: a computer in every school.

_____ 3. Gates says his reason for "tap-dancing to work" is that he enjoys making lots of money.

_____ 4. In developing countries, there are too many people who don't have the basic things they need.

_____ 5. Gates wants to give something back to the world.

_____ 6. Gates is not optimistic about the future.

Vocabulary for Comprehension

CD 2 Track 5 Read and listen to these sentences. Then circle the letter of the word or expression closest in meaning to the boldfaced word or expression.

1. Gates has been **hooked on** computers since he was thirteen. He just loves using and thinking about computers.
   a. very interested in
   b. very busy with
   c. very afraid of
   d. very disappointed by

2. The ability to read and write is **a window** into the world's knowledge. It makes learning anything possible.
   a. a computer screen
   b. a chance to receive
   c. a small period of time
   d. an opportunity to find out

3. When Gates was young, computers could **barely** do anything compared to computers today. Now computers do so much more.
   a. easily
   b. hardly
   c. surely
   d. quickly

4. Now, computers are so advanced that they can **store** thousands of photos. You can look at all your pictures anytime.
   a. buy
   b. save
   c. make
   d. lose

5. Millions of people die unnecessarily from health problems that medicines could easily **prevent**.

   a. stop from happening

   b. cause to happen

   c. maintain

   d. continue

6. New drugs can cure many **diseases** and make people healthy again.

   a. nervousness

   b. bad habits

   c. illnesses

   d. situations

7. In life, we face many **tough** problems that are hard to solve.

   a. strong

   b. weak

   c. difficult

   d. foolish

8. Gates and his wife, Melinda, spend a lot of time and money trying to help improve people's lives. They are **committed to** these goals.

   a. tired of

   b. loyal to

   c. happy about

   d. worried about

9. Gates has made great **achievements** in technology. Computers around the world use his software.

   a. failures

   b. progress

   c. successes

   d. connections

BACKGROUND NOTES

When Bill Gates was young, the "mini computers" of the 1960s were very different from our modern PCs. Individual people rarely owned these computers. They were the size of American refrigerators and cost tens of thousands of dollars (at that time). The time needed to receive information after entering data sometimes took many hours or even days.

A 1960s mini computer

Listen for Details

A CD 2 Track 6   Read these sentences. Then listen to Gates' essay again. Check (✓) the items he mentions.

☐ 1. Gates sat down at his first computer in the seventh grade.

☐ 2. Gates and Allen started Microsoft.

☐ 3. Gates and his wife created "The Bill and Melinda Gates Foundation."

☐ 4. Computers have transformed how we learn.

☐ 5. New attention is being paid to tough problems in the developing world.

☐ 6. Gates and his wife promised to help as many people as possible.

B CD 2 Track 7   Read these questions. Then listen to the essay again. Write your answers to the questions.

1. How long has Gates been working with computers?

2. According to Gates, what can computers be used to "feed?"

3. How does Gates feel about his job?

4. Gates mentions three things PCs can do that often surprise people. Name at least two.

5. Name two things Gates and his wife, Melinda, are committed to improving.

REACTING TO THE ESSAY

Discuss your answers to these questions.

1. Bill Gates feels that computers are great tools that help us solve problems that even the smartest people couldn't solve on their own. Do you agree with him? Describe ways that the computer has made the world a better place.

2. Bill Gates believes that people who are more fortunate have a responsibility to give back and help people who are less fortunate. Do you agree or disagree with him? Why?

3. Have you ever donated time or money to a charitable organization? Describe the organization, what you did, and how being charitable made you feel.

SPEAKING

In his essay, Bill Gates states his belief that creativity and the willingness to solve tough problems can make the world a better place, especially for people in need. In this section, you will create a charitable[2] organization and explain to the class the purpose of the organization and what it does.

Build Fluency

Language: Gerunds + Prepositions

A gerund is a verb that we use like a noun. To form a gerund, add -ing to the base form of the verb. To form the negative, place *not* before the gerund. Gerunds can be subjects or objects of sentences. A gerund subject is singular. Use a third-person singular form of the main verb.

GERUND AS SUBJECT	GERUND AS OBJECT
Giving back to the world *is* Gates' responsibility.	I *enjoy* **helping** people who are less fortunate.
Not improving health care *is* irresponsible.	We *understand* **not having** enough money to buy paper and pencils for school creates problems.

Use gerunds after these verbs + prepositions:

VERB + PREPOSITION + GERUND		
Verbs		**Examples**
approve of	*insist on*	Our organization *believes in* **providing** good medical care for everyone.
believe in	*pay for*	
choose between	*plan on*	
count on	*succeed in*	We *plan on* **helping** sick children
deal with	*think about*	in developing countries.

[2] generous to people who need help

Use gerunds after adjectives + prepositions, such as these:

ADJECTIVE + PREPOSITION + GERUND	
Adjectives + Prepositions	**Examples:**
accustomed to interested in bored with responsible for different from sad about excited about surprised by famous for tired of	I'm *excited about* **saving** lives in developing countries. Bill Gates is *famous for* **giving** money to charitable organizations.

PRACTICE Write the correct prepositions from the box after the underlined words. Then add the gerund form of the verbs in parentheses to complete the sentences.

about	between	for	in	~~of~~	on	to	with

1. Bill Gates has always <u>dreamed</u>   *of improving*   (improve) the world.

2. Gates believes that we should be <u>responsible</u> _____ (take care of) less fortunate people.

3. The Gateses <u>think</u> _____ (provide) better education for all children.

4. In developed countries, we are <u>accustomed</u> _____ (get) medicine as soon as we need it.

5. People in developing countries can't <u>count</u> _____ (receive) good health care.

6. These people shouldn't have to <u>choose</u> _____ (buy) food and purchasing medicine.

7. They are <u>bored</u> _____ (make) the same tough choices every day.

8. The Bill and Melinda Gates Foundation has <u>succeeded</u> _____

(help) many people in the United States and around the world.

Pronunciation: Linking Words and Sounds

> **CD 2 Track 8** Link words together to make speech sound smooth and fluent. There are several ways to link words.
>
> When the word ends in a consonant and the next word begins with a vowel, join the consonant to the vowel. Listen to the examples.
>
> EXAMPLE:
>
> believe in
> We believe in providing good medical care.
>
> When a word ends with a consonant and the next word begins with a different consonant, hold the final consonant until you are ready to say the next word.
>
> EXAMPLE:
>
> famous for
> She's famous for donating[3] money.

A **CD 2 Track 9** PRACTICE Listen and repeat the verb + preposition or the adjective + preposition.

Consonant + Vowel		Consonant + Consonant	
approve of	interested in	bored with	famous for
believe in	pay for	deal with	responsible for
excited about	plan on	different from	surprised by

[3] giving to charitable organizations

B (CD 2 Track 10) **PRACTICE** Listen to these questions and practice saying them with a partner. You will use the questions later in the unit.

1. Who are you **interested in** helping?

2. What name do you **plan on** giving your organization?

3. What does your organization **believe in**?

4. What types of services or goods will you **insist on** providing?

5. How many members will you need to **deal with** the work?

6. How much money are you going to need to **pay for** everything?

Get Ready to Speak

TASK

Explaining Purpose

In groups, create a charitable organization. Explain the purpose of your organization to the class and describe what it does.

1. Work in groups. Use the questions from the Pratice B above to help you complete the chart.

Organization name:	
Vision (Purpose):	
Responsibilities:	
Goods and services provided:	
How much money is needed:	

2. As a group, practice giving your presentation. Divide the responsibility for speaking equally among group members. Each group member should present different pieces of information. Make changes as needed.

Remember to:

- use gerunds after prepositions.
- link final consonants to the beginning of the next word if the word begins with a vowel.

Speak

Present your organization to the class. While the class listens, each student will think of one question to ask. When everyone has finished, decide which organizations your class would support. Explain why.

WRITING

Read these topics. Choose one to write about.

1. According to Gates, there are lots of ways our creativity and intelligence can improve our world. Write about one way you think we can improve the world.

2. Write about Gates' belief that people who are more fortunate have a responsibility to help people who are less fortunate. Do you agree or disagree with him? Refer to your answers from the Reacting to the Essay section on pages 68-69 to organize your details.

3. Imagine Gates will speak at your school next week. Write three questions that you plan to ask him. Explain why you have chosen these questions.

What do you believe?

As you listen to the essays in this book, think about your beliefs. Write your own *What I Believe* essay. Follow the steps on pages 127–130.

UNIT 8

THE PEOPLE WHO LOVE YOU
–Cecile Gilmer

GETTING READY

CD 2 Track 11 Listen and read about the essayist.

> ### Meet Cecile Gilmer
>
> When she was 15 years old, Cecile Gilmer went to live with the Beach family. Barbara and Roland Beach were the parents of Gilmer's best friend, Su. The Beaches treated her just like their own daughter. As a result of their care and support, Gilmer learned to believe in home, family, and herself.

Connect to the Topic

Discuss this situation with a partner.

Gilmer believes that *family* includes people who treat you like a member of their family—not just blood relatives.[1] Imagine you are having a party for all the people who have treated you like family. Whom will you invite and why?

GLOSSARY

An interstate

You will hear these words and expressions in the essay. Read their definitions before you listen.

interstate /ˈɪntɚˌsteɪt/ *n.* a major highway that goes between states

double beds /ˈdʌbəl ˈbɛdz/ *n.* beds in which two people can sleep

lunch money /ˈlʌntʃ mʌni/ *n.* money children are given to buy lunch at school

speaking lines /ˈspikɪŋ laɪnz/ *n.* spoken dialog in a theatrical play

rival /ˈraɪvəl/ *n.* a person, group, school, or organization that you compete with

insurance policy /ɪnˈʃʊrəns pɑləsi/ *n.* an agreement to pay an insurance company money regularly. The company pays you money if you or your property gets hurt.

previous /ˈpriviəs/ *adj.* happening or existing before a particular event, time, or thing

[1] biological family members

LISTENING

Listen for Main Ideas

CD 2 Track 12 Read these sentences. Then listen to Cecile Gilmer's essay. Circle the letter of the sentence that best describes the main idea.

a. Gilmer has learned to respect her blood relatives more.

b. Living with the Beaches changed Gilmer's feelings about family.

c. Gilmer went to college because she lived with the Beaches.

Vocabulary for Comprehension

CD 2 Track 14 Read and listen to these sentences. Then circle the letter of the word or expression closest in meaning to the boldfaced word or expression.

1. Teenagers often need a lot of privacy. They feel **modest** about showing their bodies and are easily embarrassed.

   a. shy   b. silly

2. Cecile Gilmer's stepmother forced Gilmer and her father to leave her house. Her stepmother was angry at her father and **kicked them out**.

   a. beat them   b. made them go

3. Gilmer was living at a Howard Johnson motel. Her best friend, Su Beach, asked Gilmer to **move in** with her family.

   a. visit   b. live

4. Su's parents agreed that Gilmer could live with them. After the Beaches **took** Gilmer **in**, she stayed with them for seven years.

   a. gave a home   b. drove far away

5. While Gilmer was away at college, the Beaches kept her room the same for her. Nothing was changed for **the entire** four years she was gone.

   a. all of   b. part of

6. The Beaches were responsible and caring. Gilmer was confident that she could always **rely on** them.

a. approve of   b. depend on

7. Su's parents helped Gilmer and Su while they were growing up. Gilmer felt she was **raised by** the Beaches, not by her father.

a. cared for   b. responsible for

8. The Beaches gave Su and Gilmer equal treatment. As a result, Gilmer no longer thinks life is **unfair**.

a. not reasonable   b. not realistic

9. When Gilmer needed help, the Beaches suddenly **showed up**. They were there when nobody else was.

a. appeared   b. called

10. As a child, Gilmer didn't trust anyone. Without the Beaches' help, she might be a **bitter** woman now.

a. generous   b. resentful

BACKGROUND NOTES

Howard Johnson's is a company that owns a group of inexpensive motor lodges (motels) and casual restaurants. They are usually next to interstates. Howard Johnson's started in 1925 and reached its biggest success in the 1960s. In 1965, Howard Johnson's made more money than McDonald's, Burger King, and Kentucky Fried Chicken combined.

A Howard Johnson's restaurant

Listen for Details

A CD 2 Track 15 Read these sentences. Then listen to Gilmer's essay again. Write *T* (true), *F* (false), or *DK* (don't know).

_____ 1. In 1977, Gilmer and her father lived in a motel room with two beds and a very small bathroom.

_____ 2. Gilmer's father had no job.

_____ 3. The Beaches only went to Sue's after-school activities.

_____ 4. The Beaches saved money for Gilmer by paying for a life insurance policy.

_____ 5. Gilmer's father tried to take care of her after her mother died.

_____ 6. Before living with the Beaches, Gilmer felt that the only person she could trust was herself.

B CD 2 Track 16 Read the chart. Then listen to the essay again. Circle the word or expression that correctly completes each statement.

General Event	Details
Gilmer and her dad lived in a motel.	1. Gilmer's dad's second marriage was (in trouble / going well).
	2. Gilmer's dad didn't know (where to take her / what to do with her).
The Beaches took Gilmer into their home, and she stayed for seven years.	3. At the Beaches, Gilmer (had to / didn't have to) make her own lunches and doctor's appointments.
	4. The Beaches gave her love and confidence by (buying her jewelry / giving her nightly hugs).

	5. The Beaches went to Gilmer's drama performance when she (had a lot of speaking lines / didn't have any speaking lines).
The Beaches took care of Gilmer even after she finished high school.	6. Cecile Gilmer and Su Beach went to rival (high schools / colleges).
	7. During her time away, the Beaches (made Gilmer's room a guest room / kept Gilmer's room the same).
	8. The Beaches (continued / stopped) paying for Gilmer's insurance policy after she finished college.

REACTING TO THE ESSAY

Discuss your answers to these questions.

1. Cecile Gilmer believes in family. How do you think she would define the word *family*? To Gilmer, what are the most important qualities of a family?

2. What are the most important qualities of a family to you? Give some examples from your family or a family you know to explain these qualities.

3. Who are some members of your family who are not blood relatives? What role do they play in your life?

SPEAKING

In her essay, Cecile Gilmer talks about her belief in family. For Gilmer, *family* doesn't mean her blood relatives, but the family who loved her—her adopted family. In this section, you will have an informal debate about bringing another child into your family.

Build Fluency

Language: Arguing a Point

Use this language to present opinions, examples, and counter opinions (opinions against someone else's opinions).

GIVING AN OPINION	GIVING AN EXAMPLE	GIVING A COUNTER OPINION
I think . . .	For example, . . .	Yes, but . . .
In my opinion, . . .	For instance, . . .	That's true, but . . .
The way I see it, . . .		I see your point, but . . .

PRACTICE Complete the conversation with expressions from the chart above. Use each expression only once. Each line stands for one word. There may be more than one correct answer.

A: Cecile Gilmer is really lucky she lived with the Beaches.

B: I think so, too. (1) _In my opinion_, they're the reason she's not bitter today.

A: What do you mean?

B: Well, (2) _____ _____, they gave her a place to live, clothes to wear, and food to eat. They treated her like their own daughter.

A: (3) _____, _____ don't you think this was probably hard on their real daughter?

B: There were advantages for Su, too. (4)_____ _____, how many kids get to choose their sister?

A: Hmm. (5) _____ _____, _____ Su might have been jealous because of all the attention her parents gave Cecile.

B: (6)_____ _____ _____ _____ _____, the situation was probably good for her.

A: I'm not so sure. (7) _____ _____ _____ _____, _____ Su was an only child. She was accustomed to having all her parents' attention. It was tough.

B: Yeah, but (8) _____ _____ it was worth it for both girls, even if living together wasn't always easy.

Pronunciation: Thought Groups

> **CD 2 Track 17** In speech, we divide sentences into short phrases called *thought groups*. Say the words in a thought group together. Listen to the example.
>
> EXAMPLE: (Cecile Gilmer) (is) (really lucky) (she lived) (with the Beaches).

CD 2 Track 18 PRACTICE Listen to the dialog in the Practice exercise on pages 80–81. Mark the thought groups with parentheses. Then practice saying the dialog with a partner.

Get Ready to Speak

TASK

Having an Informal Debate

In groups, prepare a list of possible reasons for and against taking a child into your family. Divide into teams (for or against) and have an informal debate. Then present your debate to the class.

1. Work in groups. Imagine that you have a friend in a situation like Cecile Gilmer's. Discuss reasons for and against taking that child into your family. Brainstorm reasons why this could be a good or bad thing. Look at the chart on page 82 to help you.

Reasons For	Reasons Against
1. The child might have more opportunities with you.	1. This child will probably miss his or her real family and be unhappy.
2. _____ _____	2. _____ _____
3. _____ _____	3. _____ _____

2. Divide your group into two teams: Team A is for the idea; team B is against it. In your teams, practice presenting your opinions and examples. Use the language from page 80 to help you.

3. Team A and team B get together. Practice arguing your points. Take turns presenting reasons and examples.

Remember to:

• use the expressions from page 80.

• speak in thought groups.

Speak

Have the debate. After the debate is finished, the class will discuss which point was the strongest from each side.

WRITING

Read these topics. Choose one to write about.

1. Write about Gilmer's belief that *family* includes people who treat you like a member of their family—not just blood relatives. Do you agree or disagree? Explain. Give examples.

2. Write about your answer to the Connect to the Topic section on page 75. Write about one person whom you will invite to the party. Explain what exactly this person has done to make you feel like family.

3. Write about what qualities you think are the most important in a family. Refer to the Reacting to the Essay section on page 79 to help you with your details.

What do you believe?

As you listen to the essays in this book, think about your beliefs. Write your own *What I Believe* essay. Follow the steps on pages 127–130.

UNIT 9

TOMORROW WILL BE A BETTER DAY
–Josh Rittenberg

GETTING READY

CD 2 Track 19 Listen and read about the essayist.

Meet Josh Rittenberg

When he wrote this essay, Josh Rittenberg was sixteen years old and a student at Columbia Grammar and Preparatory School in New York City. One evening, he heard his parents having a serious conversation about the future. Their conversation disturbed Rittenberg until he found some family photos. Looking at the important events in these pictures gave him hope. They helped him feel better about his chances in the future.

Connect to the Topic

Discuss these questions with a partner.

Josh Rittenberg enjoys looking at family photos. The photos give him information about the lives of his relatives. How were your parents' lives different than yours? Give two examples. Do you think life is better now than when your parents were young? Explain.

Buzz Aldrin on the moon

LISTENING

Listen for Main Ideas

CD 2 Track 20 Read the sentence and the choices below. Then listen to Josh Rittenberg's essay. Circle the letter of the answer that best completes the sentence.

According to the essay, Rittenberg is hopeful about the future because . . .

a. he trusts his parents to take care of him.

b. he is young and doesn't understand how difficult life can be.

c. he sees the ways his grandparents' and parents' lives improved.

Vocabulary for Comprehension

CD 2 Track 22 Read these words and their definitions. Use them to complete the sentences on page 87. Then listen to the sentences and check your answers.

challenge *v.* question if something was right

devastating *adj.* making someone feel extremely shocked or upset

eavesdrop (on) *v.* secretly listen to other people's conversations

generation *n.* the people in a society who are about the same age, e.g., "my parent's generation"

immigrants *n.* people who move to another country

inconceivable *adj.* too strange or unusual to seem real or possible

lousy *adj.* very bad (informal)

overheard *v.* to hear what someone is saying without planning to

the usual *n.* something that happens most of the time in most situations

1. That man was talking so loud on his cell phone that I _____ all of his private conversation. He was having a fight with his wife.

2. I was thinking about _____ stuff teenage girls think about—boys and clothes.

3. My great-grandparents and their _____ would be amazed by new inventions such as the Internet and cell phones.

4. War has a _____ effect on soldiers and ordinary citizens. It destroys so much.

5. When my parents talk at night in the living room, I sit in my bedroom and _____ on their conversations. I hear every word they say.

6. In the 19th century, millions of _____ entered the United States at Ellis Island to begin new lives. If you visit, you can see old photos of people from countries from all over the world.

7. These days people depend on computers so much that life without one is _____! We just can't imagine it.

8. You have a really _____ day when your computer crashes, your car breaks down, you are late for a job interview, and you catch a cold—all on the same day.

9. Lucas's brother thinks he knows everything. It's important to _____ him when you think he is wrong.

Listen for Details

A `CD 2 Track 23` Read these sentences. Then listen to Rittenberg's essay again. Circle the letter of the answer that best completes each sentence.

1. Rittenberg's parents were _____ about the future of the world.

   a. optimistic   b. upset   c. angry

2. Rittenberg found photos of his _____ when they were young.

   a. grandparents   b. parents   c. aunts and uncles

3. He began to think about _____ his grandparents and great-grandparents experienced.

   a. the bad things   b. the good things   c. the good and bad things

4. Rittenberg believes that his generation will see _____ changes in the world.

   a. positive   b. negative   c. no

5. Rittenberg learned the phrase "Tomorrow will be a better day" from _____.

   a. immigrants   b. his grandfather   c. his father

B `CD 2 Track 24` Rittenberg mentions both historical events his family experienced and their predictions about future events. Give examples of these events and predictions. Listen to the essay and complete the charts.

1.

	Examples
Positive Events	*vaccine for polio invented*
Negative Events	

2.

	Examples
Josh Rittenberg's parents' predictions	_____ _____
Josh Rittenberg's predictions	_____ _____

BACKGROUND NOTES

In his essay, Josh Rittenberg mentions these important events from the twentieth century:

World War I
(1914–18)
fought in Europe between the Allied Powers (France, Russia, the United Kingdom, Canada, and Italy), and Austria-Hungary, Germany, and the Ottoman Empire

1910

1920

World War II
(1939–45)
fought in Europe, Africa, and Asia between the Allies (France, Great Britain, the United States, the USSR, and China) and the Axis powers (Germany, Italy, and Japan)

1930

1940

The atomic bomb
(1945)
first (and only) nuclear weapon used

1950

The polio vaccine
(1952)
a medicine developed by Jonas Salk to prevent polio, a disease causing paralysis[1]

The Civil Rights Act
(1964)
an important law that prevented discrimination in the United States because of color, race, religion, or national origin

1960

1970

[1] loss of the ability to move your legs and/or arms

REACTING TO THE ESSAY

Discuss your answers to these questions.

1. Josh Rittenberg is optimistic about the future. His parents are not optimistic. After listening to the essay, which opinion do you agree with? Explain.

2. When he was a child, Josh's father told him, "Tomorrow will be a better day." Now his father is older, and he is afraid of the future. Why do think his father's opinion has changed?

3. When you were growing up, did you hear your parents talk about their worries? Do you think it's good for children to know their parents' concerns? Explain.

SPEAKING

In his essay, Josh Rittenberg states his belief that tomorrow will be better than today. He feels that the world of the future is going to get better, not worse. In this section, you will make predictions about the future and discuss how you think it will be better or worse than now.

Build Fluency

Language: Comparatives

To show how two people, places, or things are different, use comparatives.

ADJECTIVE COMPARATIVES	
One-syllable adjectives Adjective + -*er* cheap → cheap**er** small → small**er** <u>Note</u>: Use *than* after comparatives	EXAMPLE: Computers are **smaller** and **cheaper than** they were 50 years ago.
Two-syllable adjectives ending in -*y* -*y* becomes -*ier* easy → eas**ier** noisy → nois**ier**	EXAMPLE: Keeping in touch is **easier than** it used to be.

Two- or more-syllable adjectives	EXAMPLE:
more / less + adjective more / less crowded more / less expensive	Highways are **more crowded than** they were 50 years ago.
Irregular comparatives bad → **worse** good → **better**	EXAMPLE: Tomorrow will be a **better** day **than** today.
Not as + adjective + *as* The adjective does not change form. *Than* is not used.	EXAMPLE: Modern computers are **not as clunky as** they used to be.

PRACTICE Complete the sentences with the correct form of the adjective in parentheses. Choose between a comparative adjective or *not as* (. . . *as*).

I think the most important invention in the twentieth century was the Internet. It has made our lives better in many ways. Take e-mail, for example. It is (1) _____ (easy) than ever to stay in touch with your friends and family. E-mail is not only (2) _____ (fast) than snail mail,[2] but it's (3) _____ (not expensive), either. We don't have to buy stamps or pay for phone calls to keep in touch. E-mail is much (4) _____ (good) than snail mail. The Internet is also great for research. Using the Internet is (5) _____ (practical) than going to the library to find information. Getting information is (6) _____ (not time-consuming[3]) it used to be. All this was inconceivable to people fifty years ago. Our grandparents' lives were (7) _____ (not convenient) ours. Ordinary tasks such as cooking and washing were (8) _____ (difficult) than they are now.

[2] mail delivered by the postal system

[3] slow

Pronunciation: Stress in Compound Nouns

> **CD 2 Track 25** Compound nouns are two words that have a new meaning when they are used together or combined into one word. For example, *base + ball = baseball*. Pronounce compound nouns like single words. Stress the first syllable of the compound noun. Pronounce the vowels in both syllables clearly. Don't reduce the vowel in the unstressed syllable. Listen to the examples.
>
> EXAMPLES: BASEball   MOON shot

PRACTICE These sentences contain compound nouns. Listen and practice saying them with a partner.

1. The first American and Russian **moon shots** were in 1961.

2. I overheard my parents talking in the **living room**.

3. The world has changed a lot since my **grandparents** were young.

4. In our **lifetimes** we will see many changes, too.

5. I parked my car in the **driveway**.

6. Don't ride your bike on the **sidewalk**.

7. What are you doing this **weekend**?

Get Ready to Speak

TASK

Making predictions and comparisons

In groups, make your own predictions about the future and compare the future with the present. Discuss ways you think life will be different 25 years from now.

1. Work in pairs. Brainstorm things that make life better these days than in the past. Think about technology, fashion, science, travel, entertainment, or your own ideas. Compare them to things when your parents were young. Remember to use comparatives.

2. Predict how these same items will change in the future. Talk about the effects on people or the world these changes will have. Use *will* + the base form of the verb to make your predictions.

EXAMPLE:

"In the future, all cars will run on electricity. We will get this electricity from the sun. This will make life better because the air will not be as polluted as it is now."

3. Practice presenting your predictions. Your partner will ask you questions. Make changes as needed.

Remember to:

- use *will* + the base form of the verb to make predictions.
- use comparative adjective forms and *not as* + adjective + *as*.
- stress the first syllable in a compound noun.

> **USEFUL EXPRESSIONS**
>
> **Making sure you understand**
>
> So, do you mean . . . ?
>
> So, what you're saying is . . .
>
> (*Repeat speaker's idea.*), right?

Speak

Get together with another group. Take turns making your predictions. Then discuss the predictions. Do you agree or disagree with your group members' predictions? Explain.

WRITING

Read these topics. Choose one to write about.

1. Write your reaction to Rittenberg's statement, "Tomorrow will be a better day." Do you agree or disagree with him? Refer to your answers in the Reacting to the Essay section on page 90 to help you.

2. Look at old family photos of your parents, grandparents, or other family members. Write a description of what you see. Write what the picture says about your family's life at that time.

3. Write about some of the challenges facing your generation. Predict what will happen in the future.

What do you believe?

As you listen to the essays in this book, think about your beliefs. Write your own *What I Believe* essay. Follow the steps on pages 127–130.

WHAT HAVE I LEARNED?
–Elizabeth Deutsch Earle

GETTING READY

CD 2 Track 26   Listen and read about the essayist.

> ### Meet Elizabeth Deutsch Earle
>
> Elizabeth Deutsch Earle is a science professor at Cornell University. She has written two essays for *This I Believe.* She wrote her first essay for the original radio series many years ago. Now, after a lot of life experiences, she still believes in being a kind person, working for social justice,[1] and living in the present moment. She tries to savor each day of her life.

[1] treating everyone the same

Connect to the Topic

Discuss these questions with a partner.

Elizabeth Deutsch Earle tries to savor each moment of her day. Do you? Or do you do several things at the same time, such as talking on the phone and driving? Can you think of any advantages of only doing one activity at a time? Explain.

GLOSSARY

You will hear these words and expressions in the essay. Read their definitions before you listen.

life cycle /laɪf 'saɪkəl/ *n.* different stages of life

exceptional /ɪk'sɛpʃənəl/ *adj.* unusually good

fall short (of) /fɔl' ʃɔrt əv/ *v.* not achieve your goal

strive /straɪv/ *v.* try very hard for a long time

straightforward /streɪt'fɔrwərd/ *adj.* clear or easy to understand

savor /seɪvər/ *v.* deeply enjoy every moment of an experience

get it right /gɛt ɪt'raɪt/ *exp.* do something correctly

The life cycle

LISTENING

Listen for Main Ideas

CD 2 Track 27 Read the topics. Then listen to Elizabeth Deutsch Earle's essay. Check (✓) the topics she mentions.

☐ the present

☐ staying young

☐ her religious beliefs

☐ her achievements

☐ the unfairness in the world

☐ doing what needs to be done

Vocabulary for Comprehension

CD 2 Track 29 Read and listen to the conversation. Then match the boldfaced words and expressions with their definitions on page 98.

Justin: Grandma, can I ask you some questions? Our history teacher wants us to find out about our grandparents' beliefs.

Grandma: OK, I can do that.

Justin: Great! So then, what do you believe?

Grandma: Well, let's see. I believe that people who **prosper** in life have an **obligation** to help other people.

Justin: What do you mean?

Grandma: Well, take me for example. I have a wonderful family, a good job, plenty of food, and a safe place to live. Other people aren't so lucky.

Justin: I see. So you mean that helping people is really important.

Grandma: Right. Helping people is a **priority.** And I also believe we need to take the time to **recognize** the good things in life. You know, **get engaged in** the present.

Justin: Huh? Sorry. I don't get it.

Grandma: I mean, we need to slow down and focus on one thing at a time. We get so busy that we forget to **appreciate** the beauty around us, and that **troubles** me. Life is **precious,** and we need to savor it.

Justin: I guess you're right. Thanks Grandma!

Grandma: You're welcome.

_____ 1. prosper   a. see value in something and be thankful for it

_____ 2. obligation   b. worries or disturbs

_____ 3. priority   c. are successful

_____ 4. recognize   d. duty or responsibility

_____ 5. get engaged in   e. become very interested or involved in

_____ 6. appreciate   f. something important that gets a lot of attention

_____ 7. troubles   g. valuable and not to be wasted

_____ 8. precious   h. see or admit that something is true

Listen for Details

A CD 2 Track 30 Read these sentences. Then listen to Earle's essay again. Circle the letter of the answer that best completes each sentence.

1. Earle recorded an essay for the original *This I Believe* show over _____ years ago.

   a. 15   b. 50   c. 5

2. She still believes _____ of what she wrote back then.

   a. all   b. most   c. a little

3. She believes people who have good fortune should recognize the _____ of others.

   a. prosperity   b. value   c. needs

4. Earle tries to _____ the causes[2] that she respects.

  a. read about   b. support   c. change

5. Earle appreciates life more when she focuses on the _____.

  a. future   b. past   c. present

6. She thinks that it's important to appreciate joy _____.

  a. sometimes   b. as often as possible   c. on special occasions

B **CD 2 Track 31** Read these sentences. Then listen to the essay again. Write *T* (true) or *F* (false).

_____ 1. Since writing her first essay, Earle has graduated, gotten married and divorced, and become a famous scientist.

_____ 2. Earle worries less about the world today than she did in the 1950s.

_____ 3. By traveling in the United States and reading the news, Earle has learned that life is unfair.

_____ 4. Earle has reached all the goals she had when she was young.

_____ 5. Earle thinks people can't appreciate life when they do several things at the same time.

BACKGROUND NOTES

When she was sixteen, Elizabeth Deutsch Earle won an essay contest in her hometown of Cleveland, Ohio. The contest prize was a trip to New York City to record her essay on the original *This I Believe* radio series. The title of her first essay was "An Honest Doubter."[3] Her questioning mind and her desire to live a good and righteous life still have not changed.

Elizabeth Deutsch, left, age 16

[2] ideas that people fight for

[3] a person who asks a lot of questions

REACTING TO THE ESSAY

Discuss your answers to these questions.

1. Earle talks about the phrase "Wherever you are, be there." What does this phrase mean to you? What practical things can you do to live by this idea? Give an example.

2. Earle states that by supporting causes she respects, she only has a small effect on the world. Why do you think Earle continues to support these causes if the effect is small?

3. As we get older, some of our beliefs change. What causes them to change? Explain how one of your beliefs has changed in recent years.

SPEAKING

In her essay, Elizabeth Deutsch Earle states that it is good to spend time engaged in the present. She believes it is important to savor each day. In this section, you will prepare a radio call-in show that gives advice about savoring each day.

Build Fluency

Language: *Should, Ought to, Had better*

GIVING ADVICE	
	EXAMPLES:
To give advice, use *should (not)*, *ought to*, and *had better (not)* + the base form of the verb.	You **should** *spend* some time relaxing each day. You **shouldn't** *sit* at your desk for more than two hours without a break. You **ought to** *make* time for your hobbies.

Use *had better* to give strong advice. To soften this advice, use the adverbs *maybe* and *perhaps*.	**Maybe you'd better** *plan* your time more carefully. **Perhaps you'd better not** *put on* makeup and drive your car at the same time.
You can also use the imperative to give advice.	**Focus** on one thing at a time. **Don't do** two things at once.

PRACTICE Read the conversation from the radio show *Savor Each Day!* Rewrite the underlined sentences on the lines on page 102. Use the verbs in parentheses in the new sentences.

Host: Good morning. Welcome to *Savor Each Day!* Let's take our first caller, Elizabeth. Hi. How can we help you?

Caller: Hi. Uh, I'm a full-time university student, and I also have a part-time job. My problem is that I feel really stressed out.

Host: I see. That's tough. So <u>find some time to relax every day</u>.
(1)

Caller: And when should I do that? I don't have any free time.

Host: Here's an idea. <u>Take a short break anytime you start to feel stressed</u>. Close
(2)
your eyes for one or two minutes and just listen. Tell me, do you usually do more than one thing at a time?

Caller: Well, sure. I'm really busy. I have to do three things at the same time.

Host: So, <u>slow down and focus on one thing at a time</u>. When your mind is
(3)
focused, you won't feel stressed out.

Caller: How can I focus my mind?

Host: Well, for example, when you eat a meal, <u>concentrate on eating</u>.
(4)
<u>Don't read or watch TV while you eat</u>. <u>Eat slowly and savor your meal</u>.
(5)   (6)
<u>Take time to look at and smell your food before you eat it</u>. Enjoy it.
(7)

Caller: OK. I see what you mean. Thanks.

Host: Sorry, Elizabeth, we have another caller on the line. We have to go. Good-bye.

1. _____ (should)

2. _____ (ought to)

3. _____ (maybe/had better)

4. _____ (ought to)

5. _____ (should not)

6. _____ (had better)

7. _____ (should)

Pronunciation: Corrective Stress

CD 2 Track 32 Use stress to correct a mistake or insist that something is true. Stress the part of the sentence that you want to correct. Listen to the examples.

EXAMPLE:

A: You look hungry. You should get some lunch.

B: But I'm **not** hungry. I just ate.

Any words can be stressed, including words that are not usually stressed, such as function words (words needed for grammar but not for meaning, such as articles and conjunctions).

EXAMPLE:

A: Did you go out to dinner or to a movie last night?

B: I went out to dinner *and* a movie.

PRACTICE Listen to these dialogs. Circle the stressed words you hear in B's response. Then practice the dialogs with a partner.

1. A: Maybe you'd better use your free time to relax.

   B: I don't have any free time to relax.

2. A: You really ought to exercise more.

   B: Yeah, I need to exercise every day.

3. A: Do you usually do more than one thing at a time?

   B: I have to do three things at the same time. I'm really busy.

4. A: I'm always thinking about what I have to do next.

   B: You should only think about what you are doing at the moment.

5. A: You don't look tired.

   B: But I feel tired. I only slept three hours last night.

Get Ready to Speak

TASK

Giving Advice

In groups, prepare a role play about a radio call-in show in which callers ask for and receive advice on how to enjoy their lives more. Then present your role play to the class.

1. Work in groups. Brainstorm advice about ways to reduce stress. Complete the chart with your own ideas. Add examples.

Ways to Reduce Stress	Examples
Enjoy nature	• *go for walks* • *notice the trees and flowers*
Have fun with a pet	
Take up a hobby	

2. Create a role play of a radio call-in show. Use the chart above to help you. Divide the roles (Host, Caller 1, Caller 2, etc.).

   Remember to:

   • use *should(n't), ought to,* and *had better (not)* for advice.

   • use stress to correct mistakes and to insist that something is true.

USEFUL EXPRESSIONS	
Showing concern	**Showing you are listening**
Gee, that's too bad.	Uh-huh.
That's tough.	I see.
Oh, I'm really sorry to hear that.	Right, right.

3. Practice in front of another group. They will tell you one thing you did well and one thing that needs improvement. Make changes as needed.

Speak

Present your group's radio show role play to the class. The class will take notes on the caller's problems and host's suggestions. The class will predict which advice the caller followed.

WRITING

Read the topics. Choose one to write about.

1. Elizabeth Deutsch Earle believes in living in the present in order to savor each day. Do you think this is easy to do? Explain. Give examples. Is it practical for you? Why? Refer to the task in the Speaking section on page 103 for ideas.

2. Write about some things Earle has learned about life over the years. How she has changed? Refer to your answers from the Listen for Main Ideas section on page 97. Give examples from her essay.

3. Think about your life over the past five years. Write about how one or two of your beliefs have changed. Give examples to support how and why your beliefs have changed.

What do you believe?

As you listen to the essays in this book, think about your beliefs. Write your own *What I Believe* essay. Follow the steps on pages 127–130.

WE ARE EACH OTHER'S BUSINESS
–Eboo Patel

GETTING READY

CD 2 Track 33   Listen and read about the essayist.

Meet Eboo Patel

Eboo Patel is an American Muslim. He is the founder and director of the Interfaith Youth Core. This organization tries to create understanding and respect among people from different backgrounds. Patel believes in pluralism. He believes that people of different ethnic, religious, and cultural groups can live together in peace. He has a copy of Norman Rockwell's picture *Freedom of Worship* hanging on his office wall to remind him of his goals.

Connect to the Topic

Discuss this situation with a partner.

Eboo Patel believes that people from different ethnic and religious groups can live together in peace. Imagine this situation: You and a friend are all alone in a school hallway. Suddenly a group of tough school bullies[1] appear. They start insulting and hitting your friend because of his or her religion. What do you do or say?

GLOSSARY

You will hear these words and expressions in the essay. Read their definitions before you listen.

piety /ˈpɑiət̮i/ *n.* showing respect for God and religion

vivid depiction /vɪvɪd dɪpɪʃʌn/ *adj.+ n.* description that is so clear that it seems real

devout /dɪˈvaʊt/ *adj.* having very strong beliefs, especially religious ones

Devout Muslims at prayer

hovered /ˈhʌvɚd/ *v.* stayed close

anti-Semitic (slurs) /æntisɛmət̮ɪk(slʊrs)/ *adj. + n.* (insults) against Jewish people

averted (my) eyes /əˈvɚtd maɪ aɪz/ *exp.* looked away

---

[1] powerful people who threaten weaker people

LISTENING

Listen for Main Ideas

CD 2 Track 34 Read these sentences. Then listen to Eboo Patel's essay. Check (✓) the sentence that you think he would agree with.

☐ "Your friends should have the same beliefs that you have."

☐ "People's actions should reflect their beliefs."

☐ "People can't prevent others from suffering."

Vocabulary for Comprehension

CD 2 Track 36 Read and listen to these sentences. Then circle the letter of the word or expression closest in meaning to the boldfaced word or expression.

1. In the lunchroom, I had to sit **apart** from my best friend because his table was full.

   a. separately   b. peacefully

2. Cities have more **diversity** than towns; therefore, it's easier to meet people from different backgrounds.

   a. variety   b. problems

3. We lived in the **suburbs** of Boston, so on weekends we often went into the city.

   a. areas close to a city where people live   b. areas in the center of a city

4. There is usually a group of **thugs** in school who scare the weaker students by shouting hateful words at them.

   a. violent students   b. athletic students

5. **Confronting** bullies takes a lot of courage. You put yourself at risk.

   a. Ignoring   b. Facing

6. Last Monday, Kevin needed my support, but I didn't help him. The next day, I **avoided** him. I tried not to see him because I was embarrassed.

   a. stayed away from

   b. called on the phone

7. **Bigotry** is very painful. Nobody should be treated unfairly because of skin color, culture, or religion.

   a. Fighting

   b. Prejudice

8. When I was in high school, I **couldn't stand** being kept out of a group. Today I try to include everyone.

   a. hated

   b. regretted

9. My friend felt **abandoned**. He was disappointed his friends didn't help him when he needed it the most.

   a. embarrassed

   b. left alone

10. Getting insulted by bullies is a bad experience. When your friends don't help you, it is a **humiliating** experience.

    a. making you feel ashamed

    b. making you feel strong

CULTURE NOTES

Norman Rockwell (1894–1978) is a famous American painter. His works appeared on the cover of the *Saturday Evening Post* magazine for 47 years beginning in 1916. His paintings portrayed scenes of American life as well as his concern for social issues, such as civil rights and poverty. *Freedom of Worship* is one of four paintings in the Freedom Series, which Rockwell painted in 1942. This series was inspired by President Franklin D. Roosevelt's 1941 speech to Congress about the four freedoms: freedom of speech, freedom to worship, freedom from want, and freedom from fear.

Norman Rockwell's painting
Freedom of Worship

Listen for Details

A CD 2 Track 37 Read these questions. Then listen to Patel's essay again. Answer the questions.

1. Where did Patel attend high school?

2. How many different religions did Patel's lunchroom friends belong to?

3. What happened to Patel's Jewish friend from the lunchroom?

4. At the time, did Patel do anything to help his friend? Explain.

B CD 2 Track 38 Read these main ideas and examples. Then listen to the essay again. Match these main ideas with their examples.

Main Idea	Specific Examples
_____ 1. Patel's friends accepted one another's differences but didn't talk about these differences.	a. He avoided his friend because he couldn't stand to face him.
_____ 2. Patel and his Jewish friend didn't talk about what happened until several years later.	b. Pluralism means having the courage to act. Action is what separates a belief from an opinion.
_____ 3. Patel was humiliated by his own behavior.	c. He didn't want to come to school.
_____ 4. Patel's Jewish friend felt abandoned and scared by this bigotry.	d. They didn't explain why they couldn't eat certain food.
_____ 5. Patel learned an important lesson.	e. A few years after graduating, Patel's friend reminded him of this experience.

REACTING TO THE ESSAY

Discuss your answers to these questions.

1. After listening to the essay, has your answer to the Connect to the Topic question on page 108 changed? Explain.

2. Look at Rockwell's painting *Freedom of Worship* on page 108. After listening to the essay, why do you think Patel has this painting hanging in his office?

3. Have you ever had an experience similar to Patel's where you did not stand up for a friend? Describe the situation and how you felt afterwards.

SPEAKING

In his essay, Eboo Patel states his belief that action separates a belief from an opinion. That is, we need to practice our beliefs. Often, if we do not behave in a way that supports our beliefs, we need to take responsibility and apologize. In this section, you will role-play a situation in which you need to apologize.

Build Fluency

Language: Apologizing

MAKING AN APOLOGY	ACCEPTING AN APOLOGY	REJECTING AN APOLOGY
I'm (really) sorry for . . . (verb + -*ing*)	That's all right. . . . That's OK. . . .	Sorry, but that's no excuse. . . .
I want to apologize for . . . (verb + -*ing*)	Don't worry about it. . . .	This has happened before. . . .
I feel so bad that I (past tense verb) . . .		"Sorry" just isn't good enough. . . .

When you apologize, you should also give an explanation or an excuse.

GIVING EXPLANATIONS AND EXCUSES	
Use *had to* + the base form of the verb to explain something that was absolutely necessary.	EXAMPLE: Please forgive me, but **I had to pick** my son **up** from school because he was sick.
Use *couldn't* + the base form of the verb to explain something you were not able to do.	EXAMPLE: **I couldn't return** your book because the library was closed due to an emergency today.
When your excuse is that you didn't have the power to refrain from doing something, say *I couldn't help it*.	I'm sorry I ate your sandwich. **I couldn't help it!** I was really hungry.

PRACTICE Complete the conversations with expressions from the charts above. Use expressions only once. There may be more than one correct answer.

Conversation One

A: What happened? You're so late!

B: (1) _____.

A: You were supposed to be here 20 minutes ago.

B: I know. But as I was leaving the house, my boss called.

A: Why didn't you tell him you had an appointment?

B: I (2) _____ tell him that because he was late for a meeting and
(3) _____ ask me an important question about a report I gave him.

A: Why didn't you call me?

B: I (4) _____ call you because my husband needed to use the phone
for a business call.

A: Well, I (5) _____ tell the restaurant manager you weren't here, so they gave our table someone else.

B: Let me tell him we're here now.

Conversation Two

A: You were supposed to call me before 10:00 A.M. and now it's almost 2:00 P.M. What's your excuse this time?

B: Well, I (1) _____ finish some work and lost track of the time.[2]

A: It's always about your work.

B: I really (2) _____ this time. The deadline[3] is tomorrow.

A: (3) _____. You (4) _____ be more organized and not leave everything until the last minute.

B: Uh, I know. (5) _____ not calling you sooner. Do you want to go see a movie tonight?

A: No, (6) _____. I've already made other plans.

Pronunciation: Contrastive Stress

> **CD 2 Track 39** Stress can be moved to show contrast between two words. Stress falls on both words that are being compared. Listen to the example.
>
> EXAMPLE: You were supposed to call me at 10 in the **morning**, not 10 in the **evening**.

PRACTICE Listen and practice saying these sentences with your partner.

1. I wanted to go to the **movies**, but he wanted to go to the **baseball game**.
2. You were supposed to meet me **inside** instead of **outside**.
3. She wanted the red **roses**, not the red **tulips**.

---

[2] didn't pay attention to the time

[3] day by which something must be completed

4. I didn't order **tea**. I ordered **coffee**.

5. They wanted us to **go**, not **wait**.

Get Ready to Speak

TASK

Making Apologies and Excuses

Prepare a role play with a partner in which you make apologies and excuses. Then present your role play to two other pairs.

1. Work in pairs. Choose a situation. Then brainstorm the details of what caused one person to disappoint the other and why an apology is needed.

Situation 1

Two friends meet three years after they graduate. One of them talks about the time he was discriminated against[4] because of his religion or nationality /ethnic origin. He tells his friend how frightened and lonely he felt because nobody helped him or tried to comfort him.

Situation 2

Two colleagues are working together on a project. One is supposed to finish some work so that the other can complete his or her work. The first person doesn't do what he or she is supposed to, so the second person misses the deadline.

Situation 3

One person is always late. This person has tickets to go to the theater with a friend. She arrives 20 minutes late, and they are not allowed into the performance until the break.

2. Use the information above and the plan on page 114 to create a role play in which two people express disappointment, make apologies and excuses, and accept or reject apologies.

[4] treated unfairly

Remember to:

- use the expressions from page 110.

- use contrastive stress.

Role Play Plan

A: Express disappointment. Talk about what person B *was supposed to do*.

B: Offer an apology and an excuse. Explain why you *couldn't do* what you were supposed to or what you *had to do*.

A: Accept or reject the apology.

B: If the apology is accepted, thank the person. If the apology is rejected, try to offer more explanation.

A: Close the conversation.

3. Practice your role play in front of another pair. Each pair who listens should make a suggestion about ways the other pair could improve their role play.

USEFUL EXPRESSIONS

Expressing Disappointment

You were/weren't supposed to . . .

Why didn't you . . .

You should have called.

Speak

Present your role play to two other pairs of students. After you do your role play, listen to the feedback from your audience. See if they believed your excuses and apologies.

WRITING

Read these topics. Choose one to write about.

1. Write about a humiliating or courageous experience that strongly affected you, like Eboo Patel's experience in the lunchroom. Describe the situation in detail and how it affected you.

2. Write about Eboo Patel's belief that action is what separates a belief from an opinion. Do you agree or agree? State your position and explain your reasons.

3. Write an apology letter to the person. Use the information from your role play in the Speaking section on page 113.

What do you believe?

As you listen to the essays in this book, think about your beliefs. Write your own *What I Believe* essay. Follow the steps on pages 127–130.

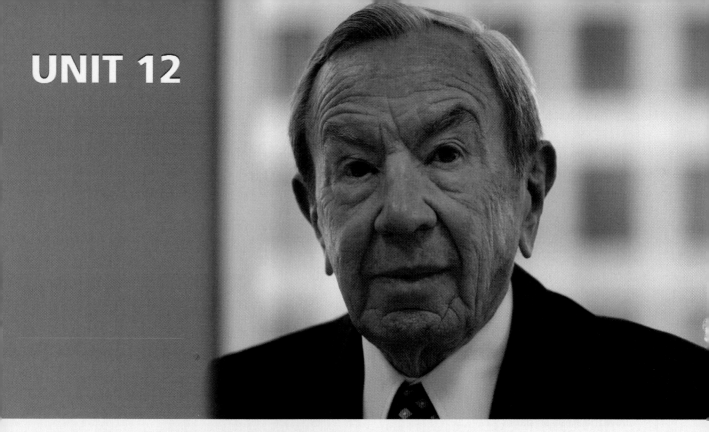

UNIT 12

A SHARED MOMENT OF TRUST
–Warren Christopher

GETTING READY

CD 2 Track 40 Listen and read about the essayist.

Meet Warren Christopher

Warren Christopher was U.S. secretary of state[1] from 1993–1997. He was also deputy secretary of state from 1977–1981 during the Iran hostage crisis.[2] His work and personal life have taught him the importance of trust. Christopher believes that we all rely on one another at some level.

[1] the U.S. official in charge of foreign relations

[2] a diplomatic crisis between the United States and Iran. See the Background Notes on page 120.

Connect to the Topic

Read the paragraph. Then complete the sentences. Discuss your answers with a partner.

Warren Christopher believes we rely on one another in many ways in our daily lives. For example, when you are driving a car, you trust that the other drivers will pay attention, stay on their side of the road, and follow traffic signals.

- If you take buses or subways, you rely on their being . . .
- If you buy food at a store or order it in a restaurant, you count on the food being . . .
- If you work, you rely on your colleagues to . . .
- If you are a student, you trust your teacher to . . .

GLOSSARY

You will hear these words and expressions in the essay. Read their definitions before you listen.

two-lane highway /tu leɪn ˈhaɪweɪ/ *n.* a highway with one road going in each direction.

double yellow line /dʌbəl yɛloʊ laɪn/ *n.* the lines that are painted on the road to show that traffic is going in opposite directions

allies /əlaɪz/ *n.* people or countries that help one another

hostage /ˈhɑstɪdʒ/ *v.* someone kept as a prisoner by an enemy, so that the other side will do what the enemy demands

transmit /trænzˈmɪt/ *v.* to send or pass something from one place or person to another

nuances /ˈnuɑnsɛz/ *n.* very small differences in meanings or feelings of words

good faith /gʊdˈfeɪθ/ *n.* honest and sincere intention

A two lane highway

LISTENING

Listen for Main Ideas

CD 2 Track 41 Read the sentence and the choices below. Then listen to Warren Christopher's essay. Circle the letter of each answer that correctly completes the sentence. Explain your choices.

Christopher states that trust sometimes requires us to _____.

    a. not do something   c. make people angry

    b. work together   d. send messages

Vocabulary for Comprehension

CD 2 Track 43 Read these words and their definitions. Use them to complete the sentences on page 119. Then listen to the sentences and check your answers.

put (great) stock in *idiom* believe in, have confidence in

face-to-face *adj.* meet with another person to talk

distracted *v.* could not pay attention

refrain from *v.* not do something

negotiating *v.* discussing something in order to reach an agreement

indispensable *adj.* something or someone who is so important or useful
      that you cannot manage without him, her, or it

cooperatively *adv.* doing something together

threat *n.* something that is dangerous

judgment *n.* ability to make a good decision

prospect *n.* something that is possible or likely to happen in the future

1. It's dangerous to talk on a cell phone and drive. People are _____ by the conversation and don't pay attention to their driving.

2. Back in the 1980s, Christopher was _____ for the release of the fifty-two Americans held hostage in Iran. This was extremely difficult because Christopher wasn't allowed to meet with the Iranian government.

3. Public transportation is _____ in a big city because many people have no other way to get around.

4. It's important to _____ speaking loudly on our cell phones so that we don't disturb others.

5. We worked on the project _____, so we had to listen carefully to one another, and it took much longer than if we had worked individually.

6. It was difficult for the foreign ministers to work together because they couldn't talk _____ and had to rely on messages only.

7. The _____ of not having electricity for more than a few hours is very scary because we rely on electricity for so many things.

8. Children _____ their parents' decisions when they are young because parents are the people they trust the most.

9. John trusted Sydney's good _____ because she had worked at the company for ten years.

10. Last Friday, I took the bus home late at night. I was a little nervous. There was no real _____, but I felt much safer when a police officer got on the bus, too.

BACKGROUND NOTES

In 1979, the former ruler of Iran, Shah Muhammad Reza Pahlevi, left Iran and entered the United States. The Shah was unpopular with many Iranians. In protest, Iranian students made hostages of ninety Americans from the United States Embassy. President Jimmy Carter took action, but fifty-two of the hostages were still not released. The hostage crisis continued for 444 days, before the fifty-two were finally set free in 1981.

Protesters with a poster of the Shah of Iran

Listen for Details

A CD 2 Track 44 Read these sentences. Then listen to Christopher's essay again. Did these things happen? Check (✓) the correct box.

	It happened.	It didn't happen.
1. A car approached Christopher from the same side of the highway.	☐	☐
2. Christopher made brief eye contact with the other driver.	☐	☐
3. Christopher was distracted by his cell phone ringing while driving.	☐	☐
4. Christopher said he has cooperated with individuals and governments.	☐	☐
5. The Iranian government agreed to negotiate with Christopher face-to-face.	☐	☐
6. The Algerian minister came to the United States.	☐	☐
7. Christopher said he doesn't believe in personal responsibility.	☐	☐

B `CD 2 Track 45` Read these questions and statements. Then listen to the essay again. Check (✓) all the statements that correctly answer each question.

1. When Christopher was driving down the dark road, he trusted the other driver would <u>not</u> do certain things. What were they?

   ☐ a. fall asleep

   ☐ b. be distracted by music

   ☐ c. drive into his lane

   ☐ d. say something

   ☐ e. talk on his cell phone

2. During the hostage negotiations, what did Christopher rely on the Algerian foreign minister to do?

   ☐ a. accept messages

   ☐ b. send messages

   ☐ c. translate messages correctly

   ☐ d. represent him correctly

   ☐ e. keep secrets

REACTING TO THE ESSAY

Discuss your answers to these questions.

1. Christopher trusted the other driver to refrain from doing certain things. In what other situations do we have to rely on others to refrain from doing something? In what situations do we have to rely on others to work cooperatively?

2. Ralph Waldo Emerson said, "Trust men and they will be true to you; treat them greatly and they will show themselves great."[3] Do you think Christopher would agree? Explain your reasons.

---

[3] *Essays, First Series:* "Prudence," 1841

3. Tell your partner about someone (such as a parent or friend) or something (such as electric power, public transportation) that you can rely on and trust. Why do you feel this way?

SPEAKING

In his essay, Warren Christopher states his belief that we all trust and rely on one another in some way. In this section, you will discuss what you would do if someone or something you rely on is suddenly not there.

Build Fluency

Language: Present Real and Unreal Conditionals

Use conditionals to talk about what happens or would happen under special conditions.

Use the present real conditional to talk about possible situations and results in the present. Place an *if* clause and result clause together. The *if* clause describes the condition, and the result clause explains what happens under this condition.

PRESENT REAL CONDITIONAL	
The simple present is used in both clauses. Note: • The *if* clause is followed by a comma when this clause is first. • You can use modals such as *can, could, should,* and *might* in the result clause.	*if* clause result clause *If* the subway **isn't** running, I **take** the bus to work. *If* I **can't listen** to my MP3 player, I **can read** a book on the subway.

Use the present unreal conditional to talk about situations that are unlikely to happen, unreal, or are imagined.

PRESENT UNREAL CONDITIONAL

	if clause result clause
The simple past is used in the *if* clause, and *would* appears in the result clause.	*If* my computer **weren't** working, I **would** go to an Internet café and use the computer there.
<u>Note</u>:	
Use *were* for first-, second-, and third-person subjects when the *if* clause verb is *be*.	*If* he were my friend, I **would send** him text messages.

PRACTICE Match the *if* clauses with their result clauses.

_____ 1. If my computer crashes,

_____ 2. If his phone is busy,

_____ 3. She would take the bus

_____ 4. If the elevator were out of service,

_____ 5. The electricity might go out

_____ 6. Jang would take his brother

to school

a. if there is a terrible storm.

b. you would take the stairs.

c. I go to the library.

d. if her neighbor couldn't give her a ride.

e. if his mother were sick.

f. I can send him a text message.

Pronunciation: Reduction and stress of *can* and *can't*

> **CD 2 Track 46** It is important to know the difference in pronunciation between *can* and *can't*. The vowel in *can* is usually reduced. *Can* sounds like /kn/. The /æ/ vowel in *can't* is always stressed and pronounced clearly. Listen to the examples.
>
> EXAMPLE:
>
>   I **can** take a bus to work, but I **can't** take the subway.
>   Use the stressed form of the vowel in short answers.
>
> EXAMPLES:
>
>   Yes, I can.   No, I can't.

A PRACTICE Listen and complete these sentences with *can* or *can't*.

1. I _____ play tennis.

2. We _____ go to the movies with you.

3. Yes, I _____.

4. Bob _____ go to the theater, and so _____ we.

5. I _____ understand what you want.

B PRACTICE Say the above sentences with a partner.

Get Ready to Speak

TASK

Sorting Alternatives

In groups, discuss who and what you, as a group, take for granted in your daily life. Talk about what you rely on them to do. Also say what you would do if they were not there for you. Then present a summary to the class.

1. Work in groups. Make a list of people and things you have to rely on to get through your daily routine smoothly.

EXAMPLE:

> I rely on the computer for word processing, to get the daily news, to do research for school, to do instant messaging, to download music, to shop, and to send and view photos.

2. Brainstorm what you could do if these people or things are suddenly unavailable.

EXAMPLE: If my computer crashed, I could

- go to an Internet Café.
- read the news in the paper or watch TV.
- go to the library to do research.
- send text messages with my cell phone.

3. Decide which person will present each point. Then practice your presentation. Your group members will tell you one thing you did well and one thing you need to improve.

Remember to:

- use the present real conditional.
- reduce the vowel in *can* and stress the vowel in *can't*.

USEFUL EXPRESSIONS

I take _____ for granted.

Without _____ life would not run as smoothly.

_____ makes my life much easier.

Speak

Get together with another group. Take turns presenting. How similar were your responses?

WRITING

Read these topics. Choose one to write about.

1. Write about Christopher's belief that we all rely on one another on some level. Do you think that is true for everyone? Explain.

2. Write about a time you had to rely on someone to refrain from doing something. Describe when this happened and where you were.

3. Imagine that someone or something you rely on is suddenly unavailable. What will you do without this person or thing? Refer to your notes from the Speaking section on page 122.

What do you believe?

As you listen to the essays in this book, think about your beliefs. Write your own *What I Believe* essay. Follow the steps on pages 127–130.

WRITE YOUR OWN ESSAY

WRITE YOUR *WHAT I BELIEVE* ESSAY

While you listen to the essays in *What I Believe 1*, you will also plan your own *What I Believe* essay. To get ready, read "What Is a Personal Essay?"

WHAT IS A PERSONAL ESSAY?

Your *What I Believe* essay is a ***personal essay***. In a personal essay, the author writes about an important belief or insight (understanding) about life. Notice the differences between personal essays, narratives, and memoirs:

Personal essay	Focuses on a ***belief or insight about life*** that is important to the writer
Personal narrative	Focuses on an ***important event***
Personal memoir	Focuses on an ***important relationship*** between the writer and a person, place, or object

Note that a personal essay often combines elements of both personal narrative and personal memoir.

WRITING TIPS

1. **Tell a story:** Talk about real events in your life or in your future dreams. Think about the specific times when your belief was formed, tested, or changed. Think of your own experience, work, and family, and tell about things you know that no one else does. Your story does not need to be heart-warming or emotional— it can be funny—but it should be real. Make sure your story is directly connected to your belief.

2. **Be brief:** Your essay will be between 350 and 500 words, about three minutes if you read it aloud.

3. **Name your belief:** Express your belief in one or two sentences. If you can't, go back and make your belief more specific.

4. **Be positive:** Have a positive attitude. Tell us what you do believe—not what you *don't* believe.

5. **Be personal:** This is a personal essay. Use in words and phrases that are comfortable for you to say. Read your essay aloud to yourself several times, and each time edit it and simplify it until you find the words, tone, and story that truly express your belief and the way you speak. Avoid using "we" to mean "people in general." Be sure that your essay is about *you*. Use the first person ("I").

YOUR *WHAT I BELIEVE* ESSAY

Follow these steps to write your own *What I Believe* essay.

☐ 1. **Brainstorm**

Make a list of beliefs: ideas, feelings, actions, or relationships that are important to you. Don't worry about grammar, spelling, or sentences.

☐ 2. **Refine**

Look at your list. Cross out ideas that you are not interested in writing about.

☐ 3. **Narrow the Topic**

Choose one belief on your list. Write one or two sentences that state your belief. Share it with a partner (or your teacher). Edit your sentences, as needed.

☐ 4. **Tell a Story**

Think of one or two true stories that help explain your belief. Be sure that the stories are directly connected to your belief.

☐ 5. **Add Examples and Details**

Add specific examples and details that make your story clearer or more interesting. Remember to focus on your belief.

☐ 6. **Organize**

Organize your ideas. Write a simple outline of your essay. Be sure your essay has a beginning, a middle, and an end.

☐ 7. **Write Your First Draft**

Write the first draft of your essay. Follow your outline in Step 6. Remember to:

☐ Write about what you believe, not what you don't believe.

☐ Write about yourself. Use the first person ("I").

☐ Use words and phrases that you are comfortable writing and saying.

□ 8. **Get Feedback**

Work with a partner. Read your partner's essay. Discuss these questions.

□ Is the belief clear and specific? Tell your partner what his/her belief is.

□ Is the introduction interesting? Tell your partner what is interesting about it.

□ Is the story directly connected to the belief? Tell your partner which parts do or do not help explain the belief.

□ Is there an interesting conclusion? Is the belief restated in the conclusion? Tell your partner what you thought about after reading the last paragraph.

□ 9. **Write Your Second Draft**

Use your partner's feedback to make changes in your essay. Write the second draft of your essay.

□ 10. **Get Feedback**

□ Read your essay out loud several times. Make changes, as needed.

□ Ask a partner to listen to you read your essay. Ask for feedback. Make changes, as needed.

□ Make a clean copy of your essay, and give your essay to your teacher for feedback.

□ 11. **Prepare the Final Draft: Your Script**

□ Look at your teacher's feedback. Make changes, as needed. Write the final draft of your essay.

□ Practice reading your essay out loud.

□ 12. **Present Your Essay**

Read your essay to your audience.

VOCABULARY

VOCABULARY MASTER LIST

Numbers refer to the units in which the items occur.

abandoned, 11
absorbed in, 1
abstract, 2
accessories, 5
achievements, 7
allies, 12
allocate, 3
anti-Semitic, 11
apart, 11
appreciate, 10
averted (my) eyes, 11
avoided, 11
barely, 7
basic needs, 7
beauty contests, 5
being open to, 6
bigotry, 11
bitter, 8
body issues, 5
bold, 1
calm, 2
camper, 5
catalog, 2
cattle, 2
challenge, 9
chore, 6
Citadel, the, 9
civil rights, 9
clunky, 7
colleague, 1
committed to, 7
confronting, 11
cooperatively, 12
corral, 2
couldn't stand, 11
countrymen, 4
cubicles, 1
Cubs, the (Chicago), 9
cultivating, 1
cured, 3
dark days, 6
defined by, 1
Depression, The Great, 9
devastating, 9
developed world, 7
devout, 11
disbelieving, 1

diseases, 7
distracted, 12
diversity, 11
do me favors, 6
domestic, 3
double beds, 8
double yellow line, 12
driveway, 6
dusty, 5
eavesdrop (on), 9
echoed, 4
entire, 8
eventually, 3
exceptional, 10
faced with, 3
face-to-face, 12
faith, 3
fall short (of), 10
fancy, 5
feedlot, 2
feminist, 5
foal, 2
followed (her) example, 4
generation, 9
genius, 1
get engaged in, 10
get it right, 10
give back, 7
gives up, 2
good faith, 12
good Samaritans, 6
got through, 3
gratitude, 6
grief, 6
hooked on, 7
hostage, 12
hostile, 4
hovered, 11
humiliating, 11
humility, 6
idols, 5
illiterate, 3
images, 2
immediate, 3
immigrants, 9
in uniform, 4
inconceivable, 9

indispensable, 12
inhabitants, 1
inhumane, 2
inspiring, 1
insurance policy, 8
interstate, 8
invisible to, 1
is all about, 5
isolation, 4
judgment, 12
keep a roof over (one's) head, 3
keep at, 1
Ken®, 5
kicked (them) out, 8
left over, 3
life cycle, 10
lousy, 9
lunch money, 8
make a difference, 5
make eye contact, 4
makes sense, 2
Malibu Barbie®, 5
medical scare, 3
modest, 8
moonshot (moon shot), 9
moron, 5
mortified, 6
move in, 8
mustered out of the army, 4
`Nam vets, 4
negotiating, 12
nuances, 12
obligation, 10
ordinary life, 1
outfits, 5
overheard, 9
pandemic, 9
parade, 4
pianist, 1
piety, 11
piled up, 6
precious, 10
pre-selected, 3
prevent, 7
previous, 8
priority, 10
prosecutor, 5

prospect, 12
prosper, 10
puff piece, a, 5
put (great) stock in, 12
raised by, 8
ranch, 2
reached out to, 4
recognize, 10
Red Sox, the (Boston), 9
refrain from, 12
rely on, 8
rival, 8
ruse, 3
savor, 10
segregation, 9
sentiments, 6
shovel, 6
showed up, 8

(side)walk, 6
slaughterhouse, 2
sleeve, 5
snowplow, 6
speaking lines, 8
speech recognition, 7
spent, 1
startled, 6
store, 7
straightforward, 10
strip mall, 1
strive, 10
submit, 3
suburbs, 11
surgical procedure, 3
surrender, 6
taken pride in, 6
tap dance to work, 7
threat, 12

thugs, 11
took in, 8
to touch, 4
tough, 7
tour of duty, 4
transformed, 1
transmit, 12
troubles, 10
two-lane highway, 12
unfair, 8
usual, the, 9
vague, 2
veteran, 4
vivid depiction, 11
warned, 4
wept, 4
window, 7
World Series, 9